WILT CHAMBERLAIN

Seven feet and one-sixteenth-of-an-inch tall, Wilt
Chamberlain is basketball's highest scorer in history and the holder of most of the NBA's individual records. Here is his spectacular career,
beginning with his high school days in Philadelphia
where he was virtually a one-man team. At the
University of Kansas he led the Jayhawks to the
highest national ratings, then left at the end of his
junior year to tour half the world with the Harlem
Globetrotters. Playing for the Philadelphia Warriors, he rapidly emerged as the game's most
prominent figure; traded to his present team,
Philadelphia's new 76ers, Wilt the Stilt at 30 continues to hold the title of basketball's outstanding
player.

This biography is both a fast-moving story of
unprecedented achievements on the basketball
court and a warm personal story of a complex
human being—supremely confident of his ability
as an athlete and at the same time a thoughtful,
sensitive young man trying to live a normal life
in the glare of public scrutiny.

GROSSET SPORTS LIBRARY

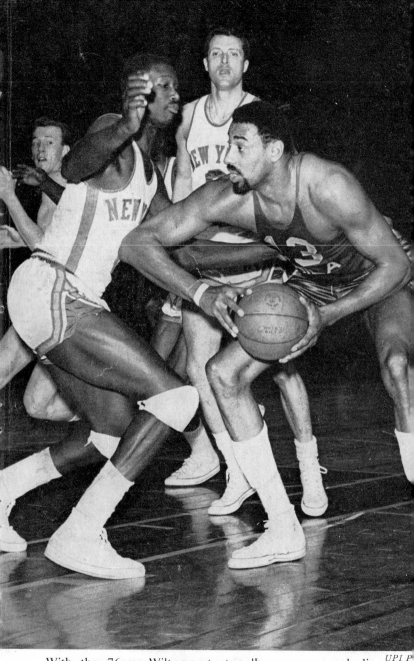

With the 76ers, Wilt resorts to elbow pressure, dueling ^{UPI P}

With a foul shot against the Knicks in Convention Hall,

Wilt Chamberlain

BY GEORGE SULLIVAN

GROSSET & DUNLAP
PUBLISHERS • NEW YORK

Contents

CONTENTS

Wilt Chamberlain

1

New Era

IT CAME DOWN to the final minutes. It almost always does in the big ones.

Through the afternoon, the Philadelphia 76ers and the Boston Celtics had battled with as much power and fury as professional basketball can produce.

The Celtics' Tom Sanders tossed in a feathery free throw and Boston went ahead, 109–108. Less than two minutes remained.

The action was under the Boston basket, and Philadelphia worked the ball into towering Wilt Chamberlain. With his back to the board, he jumped and his thin legs sprang him head high to the basket's rim. Back he reached and rolled the ball from his long fingers, but Bill Russell, another bearded pillar, was there and blocked the shot. They came down, and then like figures in a weird ballet, they jumped right back up again.

A whistle screamed. "Russell," called a referee. It

1

was his sixth personal. As he slumped to the Celtic bench, the jam-packed crowd in Boston's Garden groaned.

The teams traded free throws and the overhead electric scoreboard flashed 110–109, Boston.

The Celtics' John Havlicek, wincing with a torn groin muscle, missed a jumper from 15 feet, and Wilt's angular body flashed into the air to grab the rebound. His teammates scampered downcourt, and Wilt tilted back, like a football quarterback who had eyed an open end, and fired the ball one-handed off his ear and into the outstretched hands of a 76er.

Down the court he pounded, not with an easy grace, but terribly fast, and with legs and arms flying in every direction.

Wilt got a pass 10 feet from the basket. He jumped, falling backward as he did. With his right hand he pumped a shot that was straight, hard, deadly accurate and, from that height, as unstoppable as falling water. Now Philadelphia led, 111–110.

Havlicek tried to pass in, but his men were covered and he called time out. On the second try he got the ball to Boston corner man Sam Jones. Jones fired back to Havlicek, and Havlicek drove. Ten feet from the basket he stopped, then jumped.

Wilt was there. Waving his incredibly long arms, he rendered Havlicek's lethal jumper no more harmful than a water pistol. The shot went wide and it was Wilt who grabbed it. He was fouled. Two shots.

There were nine seconds remaining as Chamberlain stood at the foul line waiting for the ball from the referee. The Boston fans were strangely, almost ominously, silent.

Two misses—and for Wilt Chamberlain two free throw misses are not a rare occurrence—and it would be Boston's ball and the Celtics would have a chance to tie it.

Wilt stood at the foul line and sighted his target. His lungs burned for air and he showed the pain. Sweat poured down his face and trickled in drops from his goatee.

Shooting underhand, with a great dip in his knees, he lofted the ball up. It touched neither the backboard nor the rim. It was perfect. The second shot was perfect too.

The game was won. The Philadelphia 76ers were propelled into first place in the standings of the Eastern Division of the National Basketball Association over the crumbling Boston Celtics. Never before in the past nine years had any other team but the Celtics led at this waning stage of the season.

"The Celtics are dead!" "They are dead, man!" "They are dead!" came the shouts from the Philadelphia dressing room. The game had helped to wipe out many seasons of bitter memories.

Wilt Chamberlain, slumped on a bench in front of his locker, his uniform as wet as if he had worn it in a shower, was less boisterous than the rest. In seven long and often grim years as a professional, he had never felt so close to a championship. Always before it had been plucked away. He wasn't going to celebrate—not yet.

2

"The Perfect Instrument"

IT WASN'T VERY many years ago that the score of a
basketball game was hardly ever more than 30 points.
In 1926, City College of New York lost to Carnegie
Tech, 13–12. In another game of the time, City defeated Temple University, 15–14.

Wilt Chamberlain did not change this, but a young
man named Hank Luisetti did.

Strong, slim and dark-haired, Luisetti played for
Stanford University and came to prominence first on
the West Coast where newspapers enthused about his
matchless skills as a passer and a dribbler and his
blinding speed. But what made him a sensation was his
one-handed shot, which earned him an average of 22
points a game, unbelievable in a day when there was a
time consuming center jump after every basket.

Despite Luisetti's success in the West, fans in the
East, particularly in the New York City area, where the
country's best college teams of the time were centered,

were skeptical of the glowing reports about the tall and rangy young man. (Luisetti stood 6 feet 3 inches; in the mid-1930's that was considered tall.) Players and teams from other parts of the country had been held in just as high esteem as Luisetti and the Stanford Indians, but when these pretenders were matched in Madison Square Garden against one of the local powerhouses, they invariably folded.

Stanford's test came on the night of December 30, 1936, when they faced Long Island University at the Garden. Coached by the fiery Clair Bee, LIU owned a wondrous 43 game winning streak. The team dazzled the opposition with its ball handling, and they boasted players who were artists in the execution of the set shot, the most formidable weapon of the day. The shooter gripped the ball firmly with two hands, balanced himself solidly on both feet, and then fired.

LIU took a quick lead as the game got underway, and the New York fans settled back to watch the hometown team add to its string. But Bee's charges did not stay ahead for long.

Luisetti began to fire. On the run, he would push a soft one-hander and, more often than not, it would go in. The crowd was unbelieving. And it was not only Luisetti; other players on the team had the same deft talent.

The LIU winning streak came to an end that evening, but so too, and much more significantly, did Eastern style basketball. In a thousand gymnasiums and playgrounds throughout the country, youngsters began to imitate the graceful one-handed lob of Hank Luisetti. Basketball had turned a corner.

When professional basketball began to take hold in the mid-1940's, the push shot was an accepted fact of life, and so were high scores. In the deciding game for the NBA Championship in 1947, the Philadelphia Warriors downed the Chicago Stags, 83–80. Joe Fulks of the Warriors led all of the professional players that year with a 23.2 average per game. The most points he scored in one game that season was 41, also a league high.

In the years that followed, scores remained pretty much in that area with one exception. That exception was the bruising and spectacled George Mikan, who burst upon the professional scene in 1948. Mikan's average for the first three years of the six he played approached 30 points a game. The closest he came was in 1949 when he averaged 28.3.

In 1955, with Mikan in retirement, scores settled back to what they had been a decade before. Teams would break the 100-point barrier now and then; however, individual averages were about what they had been when Joe Fulks was leading the way.

Now another change came, this one in the rules. In 1956, the National Basketball Association introduced the 24-second clock, which obliged a team to shoot within that space of time or lose the ball to the opposition. By forcing players to take shots, it raised scores, but contrary to common belief, it did not raise them spectacularly. The greatest effect the clock had was to make basketball a much faster game.

Another reason for high scores today—and no doubt the prime reason—is the players themselves. Professional basketball draws its teams from the highest scoring players of college basketball. "These players, as they mature, reach the epitome of their skills," says Walter Kennedy, President of the National Basketball Association. "They develop shots that are uncanny—that defy normal defense."

Of course, behind all of this—behind the institution of the 24-second clock, and behind the unstoppable offensive skills the players seek to cultivate—lies the public's preference for high scores.

All this was in the background on that October evening in 1959 when Wilton Norman Chamberlain, just past 23, wearing No. 13 on his fluorescent blue and red-trimmed Philadelphia Warriors uniform ambled out onto the gleaming court of Madison Square Garden to make his professional league debut. Unfortunately for them, the New York Knickerbockers furnished the opposition.

Bob Pettit of the St. Louis Hawks had led all professionals in scoring the year before Wilt joined the Warriors. Pettit had established an all-time record with a then gaudy 29.2 points a game. In setting the mark, he became the first player to top Mikan's 28.4 average set back in 1951.

In the season before Wilt's debut, Elgin Baylor of Minneapolis had recorded the highest number of points in a single contest. He had netted 55 in a game against Cincinnati.

That night against the Knicks in his premiere professional game, Wilt scored 43 points. He performed with great distinction as rebounder and, all in all, was judged to be a sensation. Seldom since has he been anything but.

In his rookie year, Wilt averaged 37.6 points a game. He not only broke Bob Pettit's record, he shattered it. It was as if Roger Maris had smashed Babe Ruth's home run mark, not by hitting 61 home runs, but by blasting 79 of them.

In his second year in professional basketball, Wilt showed slight improvement and his average climbed to 38.4 points a game. His next year, the 1961–1962 season, was his best. He averaged 50.4 points per game.

No one had ever averaged 50 points per game over an entire season as Wilt did in 1961–1962. No one had even averaged 40 points. Only a very small handful had ever averaged 30.

That season he scored more than 4,000 points.

Consider this fact: Only five other players in the league scored *half* as many points as Wilt did that season, and not one player of these five came within 1,500 points of Wilt's total.

The Official Record Book of the NBA lists the 33 times a player has scored more than 60 points in a single game; 27 of those times the player's name was Wilt Chamberlain. Once—incredibly—he scored 100 points in a game. No one has come within miles of that mark.

Name any arena in the country—the Boston Garden, Cobo Hall in Detroit, the Los Angeles Sports Arena, Madison Square Garden. If Wilt has played there, the chances are 99 out of 100 he holds the scoring mark.

It is not just in field goal-making he has won eminence. He has taken more shots, grabbed more rebounds, averaged more minutes per game (the "Iron Giant" he has been called) and drawn more fouls than any other player in the whole history of basketball. Without Wilt's name on its pages, the thick NBA record book would be only a flimsy booklet. Jim Murray, of the Los Angeles *Times,* has observed, "The only thing Wilt Chamberlain can't do with a basketball is eat it."

Wilt's ability to cram a 30 inch ball into a 56 inch hoop has also enabled him to smash professional basketball's salary records. When he entered the NBA, there was a $25,000 ceiling on salaries. Wilt broke through this barrier his first year. And through the influence he has brought to bear, owners have developed a brand new concept toward what they pay their stars. Even $50,000 salaries are no longer considered remote; Bill Russell of the Boston Celtics earns twice that.

His influence has been great; his pre-eminence is even greater. No athlete, it is safe to say, has ever dominated any sport the way Wilt Chamberlain has come to dominate professional basketball.

Reports vary but it is a matter of fact that Wilton Norman Chamberlain stands 7 feet $\frac{1}{16}$ of an inch tall.

When you speak to Wilt, it is not enough to simply look up; you must tilt your head back, just as if you were reading a street sign. When he was 15 years old, playing high school basketball, he was already 6 feet 10 inches tall, and he could look down upon teammates and opposing players as if he were on a stepladder.

In any group Wilt stands out. Even among professional basketball players, where to be 6 feet 8 inches is not considered out of the ordinary, Wilt's head pokes above the rest. Coach Frank McGuire of South Carolina saw Wilt as a college player and described him as "a tree surrounded by bushes."

Wilt's legs are thin and his hips are narrow. His chest is broad, his shoulders wide and his arms well-muscled—not knotted, but with slender muscles like those of a track star.

From finger tip to finger tip, Wilt is 101 inches. He has a standing reach of 9 feet 7 inches, just a few inches below the basket's rim.

Wilt's hands are immense. If you were to shake, your hand would be swallowed up in his. His face is long and it looks longer because his chin is tufted with a short and pointed beard.

Wilt's height only partially explains his success. There have been other Goliaths in basketball, other players who have been 7 feet tall or very close to it. Ray Felix, Walt Bellamy and Nate Thurmond each measured 6 feet 11 inches. Walt Dukes and Bob Kurland were 7 footers. Swede Halbrook, who played for Syracuse early in the 1960's, was 7 feet 3 inches. Yet not one of these performed with Chamberlain's wizardry.

Wilt's superiority is due, first of all, to the fact that he is a splendid athlete—a young man blessed with great quantities of physical strength, skill, stamina and speed. It so happens this athlete is slightly more than 7 feet tall.

In other words, Wilt's size ordained he would become a basketball player. His prowess as an athlete has made him a great one.

Wilt, who weighs 270 pounds, is one of the strongest men in sports and one of basketball's fastest runners. He has terrific reflexes, a high jumper's leg spring and unusual balance for a man so large.

Next to basketball, Wilt's first love is track, and field. In high school his skills carried him to marks of 48.8 in the 440, and 1:58.6 in the 880. He reached 22 feet 8 inches in the broad jump, and 53 feet 4 inches in the shot-put. He also ran cross country. As a college sophomore, in a Big Eight Indoor Track Meet, he cleared 6 feet 6¾ inches in the high jump, good enough to gain a tie for first place in the event.

Wilt, in fact, excels in every sport where the emphasis is on the individual—weight lifting, bowling and wrestling. Hand-wrestling, too. "Wilt's the only man I ever hand-wrestled that I couldn't beat," said Bill Neider, the muscled Olympic shot-putting champion.

You must watch Chamberlain to appreciate his immense skills—his terrible quickness, his tremendous reach and extraordinary spring.

Watch him twist, turn and feint with fluid speed. Often there is no way to stop him. He can leap and take a pass at 12 feet—where no one else can possibly stretch—and stuff the ball down into the basket, down with pile driver force.

Watch him drive to the top of the keyhole for what looks to be a one-handed jump. He springs up, but he doesn't come down; he floats toward the basket, his body twisting in the air as he gains position for the shot. Often he lands somewhere in back of the basket. Or he can hook (though he disdains the shot in favor of the jumper), his arm sweeping like a giant scythe, and the ball arcs, untouchable, over the upstretched hands of the defenders.

Johnny Castellani, coach of the Minneapolis Lakers (now the Los Angeles Lakers) during Wilt's rookie year, was wide-eyed the first time he saw Chamberlain in action. "He's devastating; he's fantastic," Castellani said. "He gets the ball and goes right over you."

There is a tendency to underestimate Wilt's defensive skills though these, too, are much above the ordinary.

When Wilt guards a basket, no shot from in close has much of a chance. He bats away lay-ups; jump shots get blocked, and even set shots and long one-handers are not Chamberlain-proof.

Wilt's mere presence on the court serves to intimidate opposition shooters. Not just the man he is guarding but every rival player must be aware of where Chamberlain is before he passes or takes a shot.

Wilt's greatness as a basketball star has been achieved in the face of certain playing deficiencies. He would win no trophies as a dribbler; he is only average as a passer. Whole reams of copy have been written about his shortcomings as a free throw shooter. Yet he has attained his eminence in spite of these inadequacies, and it is further testimony to his skills that he has.

No coach has ever found a way to successfully and consistently cope with Chamberlain. Technical means have been suggested, like raising the baskets two feet, or even three, or eliminating the dunk and all other shots initiated above the basket's rim. Chances are these innovations would not change things very much. The Dipper would find a way to contend with such harassment.

The massive presence of Wilt Chamberlain has come to overshadow the early deeds of Hank Luisetti and George Mikan and the immutable blink of the 24-second clock. He has picked up the game of basketball and shaken it by the scruff of the neck, and the game will never be the same because of him. And he has done this because he is, as one of his teammates once called him, "The most perfect instrument God has ever made to play basketball."

3

Haddington

TODAY, legions of Wilt's admirers and many of his detractors, too, claim he *was* born to play basketball. Yet his early life—before he turned into his teens, at least—gives only the slightest evidence that this might have been true.

Wilt was born on August 21, 1936, in Philadelphia. Not exactly in Philadelphia, it must be said. Instead, in West Philadelphia. And *West* Philadelphia is quite different.

He was of normal size and weight.

His father, Bill, and his mother, Olivia, were 5 feet 9 inches, and 5 feet 10 inches, respectively. However, his mother's father was tall, extremely tall—7 feet, or very close to it. But a number of years were to go by before anyone realized how profoundly Wilt's grandfather was to influence him, genetically speaking.

Wilt had two brothers and six sisters, and his father worked at the Curtis Publishing Company in Philadel-

13

phia. His father's pay was steady and it provided the Chamberlain family with the basics—food, clothing and shelter—and not much else. They were not poverty stricken, but they were not well-to-do by any means.

Neighbors remember Wilt's parents as fine church-going people, and Wilt and his brothers and sisters were taught early the meaning of right and wrong.

The Chamberlains owned an eight-room house at 401 North Salford Street in the Haddington section of West Philadelphia. Any visitor to Haddington would recognize immediately that the section bore two characteristics:

First, it was a Negro section.

Second, it was composed of that peculiarly Philadelphian institution of two-story attached houses called "row houses." Over West Philadelphia, row houses stretched block after block for mile after mile. And on each block the houses were of the same precise architectural style. They looked like lines of soldiers standing at roll call.

Though crowded, the neighborhood was neat and clean, and it was extremely urban. In front of the span of row homes extended a strip of concrete sidewalk. In front of the sidewalk was the asphalt street. Haddington was virtually treeless. Children, in fact, were about the only growing things.

The Chamberlains did not live in a typical row house. They owned one-half of what in local parlance is called a "semi-detached." This term refers to a pair of two-story houses joined together by a common interior wall. These partnered dwellings extended the length of North Salford Street.

The dwellings were of gray brick and shingle, and over the front porch of each slanted a shingled roof. These porch roofs, one adjacent to the other and separated by several feet, provided young Wilt with one of his early forms of recreation. Neighbors of the Chamberlains hold vivid memories of Wilt climbing to the porch roof of his own home, a corner house, and then leaping gazelle-like across the yawning gap to the porch roof of the adjoining house, and then to the house adjoining that, and so on, down the entire city block. Porch-jumping is a rare sport, indeed, but even as a pre-teen youngster, Wilt's legs were long and limber enough to relieve the pastime of its precarious nature.

When Wilt was about 10 years old his height earned him his nickname. "I was always bumping my head in doorways and places where the ceiling was low," he once recalled. One day when he was playing in an empty house, he ran into a low-hanging length of pipe and gave himself a black eye.

His friends kidded him about it, and they told him he should "dip under" whenever he came to something low. They started to call him "The Dipper." Later it became "Dippy" or "Dip."

He was tall all right, but not so tall he made people gawk—not yet. Neighbors felt he was probably going to grow to be about the same height as his brother Wilbert, who sprouted to 6 feet 6 inches.

There were other sports besides porch-jumping. At the George Brooks Elementary School, where Wilt's teachers remember him as "well-liked and well-behaved," he played dodge-ball on the concrete playground and a variety of chase games. After school or on weekends, wall-ball, a type of handball played off the side of a house, was a favorite.

Stickball, a sport relished by most big city youngsters, was never much in vogue. The streets of West Philadelphia were too narrow for the game and further narrowed by the cars that parked on them. And since the Chamberlains lived near a huge garage for city buses, the main thoroughfares were always busy with the vehicles coming and going and intruding upon play.

Basketball? Basketball came later. When Wilt was an elementary school youngster, he had only the slightest interest in the sport. He considered it something of a sissy game.

In the United States before World War II, Negro youngsters did not pursue the sport of basketball to any discernible degree. There was little reason for them to. Certainly not on a professional basis and only to a limited degree as a collegian was there any future in sport for the Negro player.

Late in the 1940's, change came. Branch Rickey brought a fellow named Jackie Robinson into major league baseball and age-old barriers began to be lifted. Much more important, a Negro woman in Montgomery, Alabama, decided she wanted to sit in the *front* of the bus, and Martin Luther King agreed she should be allowed to. A vast social upheaval was beginning.

For the Negro youngsters of Haddington and every other part of the United States, all of a sudden there became a reason to play basketball. There *was* a future in it—a chance for a college scholarship, and after that maybe an opportunity to play professional ball.

With the zooming interest came facilities to play the game. Not far from Wilt's home, the Camphor Memorial Church built a court. Then the Greater St. Matthews Church followed with another one. In 1949 the Department of Recreation of the City of Philadelphia built Haddington Center at 57th Street and Haverford Avenue, for Wilt a five-minute spring from his house on Salford.

An oasis in a concrete and asphalt wasteland, Haddington Center offered organized programs in tumbling, modern dance, ceramics, volleyball and basketball—mostly basketball. It was Haddington Center that really triggered the sport's boom in Wilt's neighborhood.

To use the word "boom" is not to overstate the

situation. Indeed, almost every youngster began to play the sport.

They learned well. Today, Blinky Brown, one-time Recreation Leader at Haddington Center and later an instructor in Physical Education at West Philadelphia's Overbrook High School, can make a statement like this: "Youngsters you round up on almost any street corner in West Philadelphia would make high school All Americans anywhere else."

This statement is something of an exaggeration. Then again, it may not be. Today the ranks of professional basketball are liberally sprinkled with players who followed the Haddington-Overbrook route to stardom. There was Jackie Moore who played for the Philadelphia Warriors. Then came Wilt. Then Wayne Hightower of the San Francisco Warriors. Then Walt Hazzard of the Los Angeles Lakers and, most recently, Wally Jones, a teammate of Wilt's on the 76ers. There will be others. West Philadelphia has become to basketball almost what the coal-mining districts of Pennsylvania were to football not so long ago.

By the time Wilt reached his sixth and final year of elementary school, he was no longer simply tall, he was conspicuously so. He had to crouch down to get through the doorway of his classroom. He towered over storage cabinets and bookcases and he had to sink in the knees to write on the blackboard.

In junior high school, he continued to shoot skyward. One summer he vacationed with his father's relatives in Laneview, Virginia. When he returned home his friends were astonished; he had exploded four full inches.

At home Wilt's height was beginning to cause difficulty. His father had to go around the house and raise all the chandeliers and light fixtures.

Getting clothing that fit was another problem. He outgrew his trousers and shirts almost before his mother could get them home from the store. He slept in a standard size bed, but he had to roll himself into an "S" shape in order to be able to do so.

His height was also becoming something of an emotional problem to him. The stares he attracted everywhere he went were beginning to make him self-conscious. He realized people felt awkward in his presence, unsure of how to act. He realized people considered him abnormal—a freak. And, worst of all, there was no escaping it.

At times he seemed smart-alecky, but it was just a cover up against his fear of being embarrassed. With strangers he was invariably aloof, and for the same reason.

Naturally, Wilt became caught up in West Philadelphia's surging interest in basketball. His size made that inevitable. It was while attending Shoemaker Junior High School that he got his first taste of the sport.

On the basketball court no one stared at him. Instead his height was praised and applauded. Quickly basketball became Wilt's consuming interest.

He played at school. He played every day after school.

Saturday mornings he might earn some pocket money by delivering orders for Ben's Grocery and for a while he worked part-time at a neighborhood motion picture theatre, but invariably he would wind up the day at Haddington Center for a fast scrimmage or a game.

Wilt has never forgotten Haddington Center, nor have the center personnel forgotten him. In 1960 they established a Wilt Chamberlain Award, and it is presented each year to the youngster who shows the most outstanding qualities of "leadership, service and participation." If Wilt's schedule allows, he personally makes the award presentation.

There were many, many people who helped Wilt develop as a player. Jackie Moore, who achieved basketball stardom at La Salle College, in Philadelphia, and later with the Philadelphia Warriors, was one of the first.

Vic Harris was also one of Wilt's early coaches at Haddington Center. Then came James "Blinky" Brown. As Blinky is quick to point out, "No one man made that boy. Many, many contributed."

Wilt was competing in a church league. He played on a YMCA team and in the Police Athletic League. He played on a team that represented Haddington Center in Recreation Department competition, and on another in a junior high school league. Everywhere he picked up bits and pieces of technique and strategy.

When he first began the sport, he was a gangling youngster and not very strong.

"His legs were very thin and it didn't seem they could carry him up and down the court," Blinky Brown recalls. "In fact I had a fellow once bet me that Wilt would never be strong enough to make college ball.

"One of the good things about him was that he'd always listen to his coaches. He'd listen carefully, but he'd always make up his own mind about what he was going to do.

"At first he was a little too timid for the game. And he took a lot of punishment because of it.

"If you chucked an elbow in his ribs, he wouldn't elbow you back. What he'd do would be to block your shot. That was his way of retaliating."

But even in these embryonic days of his career, Wilt's future was being forecast. Everyone put him in a "can't miss" category.

He was beginning now to attract attention in his neighborhood. Folks asked who was that great big boy with the long legs walking down Haverford Avenue and bouncing a basketball.

Shortly everyone would know.

4

"The Stilt"

WILT WAS ONE MONTH past his sixteenth birthday when he entered West Philadelphia's Overbrook High School. But he was a 16-year-old the likes of which few people have ever seen.

He stood a towering 6 feet 11 inches, and he weighed 202 pounds. His growth had slowed some, but he wondered if it was ever going to stop.

He wore a size 13 shoe, a 17 collar and he had a 39 sleeve. In his basketball uniform, he looked 6 feet 11 inches at the very least. His spindly arms and his pipestem legs—especially his legs—were his most striking characteristics.

Jack Ryan, who covered high school sports for the Philadelphia *Bulletin,* scouted young Chamberlain when he was playing for Shoemaker Junior High School, and it was Ryan who tagged him "Wilt the Stilt."

"With that big torso atop those long thin legs, he

20

looked just like a man on stilts," Ryan recalls. "The name came to me the first time I saw him."

The name was to stick to Wilt the rest of his playing days, but he has never liked it. "It sounds like some kind of an ugly bird," he says. He much prefers to be called "Dip" or "Dipper."

Basketball, of course, was his great passion, but he was interested in other sports. He planned to pursue both track and swimming at high school, sports he felt would build his stamina and improve his coordination.

His studies were also important to him. He had a deep realization that high school was meant to prepare him for college educationally. He knew he was going to become thoroughly immersed in basketball, but he made up his mind that he would not become so absorbed in the sport his studies would suffer.

Thanks to his height and to the long hours of competition at Haddington Center, at Shoemaker Junior High and at the Christian Street YMCA, and most any other place the young man could toss a ball at a hoop, Wilt was a skilled performer by the time he entered Overbrook High School. Wilt's freshman coach, Sam Cozen, now basketball coach at the Drexel Institute of Technology in Philadelphia, reflected a widely held opinion when he declared that Wilt figured to be, "The best player ever to come out of these parts."

Even at 16, Wilt was magnificent to watch. He had lost much of his early awkwardness and he amazed observers with his mobility and dexterity.

His best shot was his jumper, of course. Because of the height at which it was delivered, it traveled like a line drive. He banked it off the backboard, in fact, he banked in almost every close-up shot.

Dunking posed no difficulty for him. He could stand flat-footed and come within less than an inch of touching the basket rim. Of course, a number of professional players can equal this attainment, but Wilt, whom one writer dubbed "The Hook and Ladder," could do it at 16.

His often hapless court adversaries would stand open-mouthed in pre-game warm-ups and watch Wilt cram the ball through the basket with one hand and catch it with the other after it had swished through the net. Or he would go up with a ball in each hand and while in mid-air, he would slam both through, one after the other.

On defense, Overbrook used a zone and Wilt "played" the basket, though in addition to batting away shots that came close to the rim, he could move out quickly to block a shot. He seldom fouled out—a talent he displays to this day.

Wilt was a wonder, too, as a rebounder. "He knew the angles; he almost always knew the way the ball was going to bounce," says Cecil Mosenson, who coached Wilt at Overbrook High during Chamberlain's junior and senior years. Wilt preferred, of course, to grab the ball with both hands, but when he had to, he could leap and snatch it from the boards with either his right or his left. His hands could control the ball the way those of an average size player might control a softball.

Wilt's high school coaches worked to embellish his many-sided skills. "All the fundamentals he knew," says Mosenson. "We worked to improve his moves in the pivot or his positioning on rebounds. We worked on the fast break. Things like that.

"Wilt had unusual coordination to go with his size and strength," states Mosenson, now basketball coach at Upper Moreland High School near Philadelphia. "He had great stamina, too. He could run all day.

"When he was in high school, people used to compare him with Tom Gola, and say that some day he was going to be as fine a player as Gola became. I thought this was silly. Gola is a skillful professional all right, but you could see that Wilt was going to be the greatest."

In games where the Overbrook team built an early and lopsided lead, Mosenson would play Wilt only during the first half, so the score would not swell, embarrassing the opposition. But in close games and in scrimmages Wilt would play without a break.

The standard defense against Wilt was to triple-team him or even quadruple-team him. In his first year at Overbrook, Wilt led the team to the Public League or city high school championship, but then they lost to West Catholic in the Inter-League or all-city play-offs.

In preparing for the game, the West Catholic coach had one of his youngsters stand atop a table placed at the foul line, as a sort of mock-up of Wilt. Then the coach had four of his players guard this imitation Chamberlain, jumping up and all around the table to block passes, waving their hands in his face and generally doing everything they could think of to bedevil him. This planning and its execution, combined with the inability of Wilt's teammates to score from the outside, cost Overbrook the game.

The following year it was a different story. Overbrook went through a 20 game season without a single defeat and climaxed the year by winning both the Public League and Inter-League titles. Wilt turned in a superb season, and his play caused Jack Ryan of the Philadelphia *Bulletin* to comment, "The only way to stop Chamberlain is to have him forget to show up for the game."

The game for the Public League Championship was played in Philadelphia's Palestra before almost 6,000 wildly screaming youngsters. Northeast High was the rival. When the final buzzer sounded, Overbrook's cheerleaders and a sprinkling of fans rushed to Chamberlain and tried to jack up his 6 foot 11 inch frame onto their shoulders. They got him part way up but then he slipped from their collective grasp and sank ingloriously to the floor. He was just too big and tall.

In the Inter-League championship game, Overbrook again faced West Catholic. Wilt was in excellent form. Though mauled continually throughout the game, he maintained his aplomb to score 32 points and thereby tie a play-off record. He easily won the game's outstanding player award. But this time Wilt did not have to shoulder the whole burden. When the defense collapsed upon Wilt as they had the year before, inevitably the cornermen were left unguarded. This time they plunked away at the basket and their outside shooting broke up the game early.

Wilt's performances at Overbrook High demonstrated that while he might sometimes be classed as brilliant, he was not superhuman. He could not win games all by himself. Dozen of times in the years to come, teammates, coaches, owners, fans and newspaper writers would expect him to.

Though he was thoroughly engrossed in basketball, Wilt also won some stature for himself in track and field. Ben Ogden, Overbrook's track coach, was thrilled by the young man's fluid nine foot stride.

When he was 16 years old, he set a number of AAU junior records. Competing for a Police Athletic League (PAL) track squad, he ran the 440 in 48.8. At the time, such an achievement would have ranked as a high school record, but it was not run in championship competition and had to be in order to win official sanction. When Wilt was 15, he ran the 880 in 1:58.6.

During his second year at high school, Wilt somehow found time to lead the Christian Street YMCA basketball team to the national YMCA title. As a senior at high school, he led Overbrook in a sweep of both the Public and Inter-League championships for the second straight year.

Wilt shattered every high school scoring record. Once he scored 73 points in a game; twice he scored 90 points. In games like these, the opposition did little more than stand around and watch Wilt perform.

Overbrook lost only three games in the three years Wilt played for the team, and during that time, he scored an amazing 2,252 points, an average of 37 points a game. Tom Gola, with 2,222 points, had held the record, but Gola's total was accrued over four seasons, not three.

Beginning with his second year at high school, Wilt's amazing talents began to attract nationwide attention. *Sport* Magazine featured him in an article entitled "The High School Kid Who Could Play Pro Ball Now." Soon other magazines began saying the same thing.

Indeed, the pro teams already had Wilt spotted, and Eddie Gottlieb, who owned the Philadelphia Warriors in the National Basketball Association, dreamed of the day Wilt might play for him. At length he thought of a way to make his dreams come true.

Early in 1955, in a meeting of NBA owners in New York City, Gottlieb was successful in getting a bit of legislation through that has come to be known as the "Chamberlain rule." It specified that teams could lay claim to players who were high school seniors. Of course, teams could only claim players within their geographical area. A high school star so claimed could then be drafted by the team when the youngster's college class graduated.

Most of the NBA owners were in favor of the idea. There were other 7-footers in cities where NBA franchises were located, and the owners of these franchises were very interested in corraling local stars. Despite opposition from the New York Knickerbockers, Gottlieb's "bill" passed, and with its passage Wilt's future as a professional was pretty well decided. It was now assured that Eddie Gottlieb and his Warriors had first claim on him, and it was a certainty that Gottlieb would exercise the claim.

Still, Gottlieb could not rest easy with complete confidence that Wilt was Philadelphia property. The new rule also stipulated that if the player claimed decided to attend a college within the territorial area of another team—that is, within a 50 mile radius of another team—the claim was to be voided. So if Wilt chose to go to Harvard, the Boston Celtics would have a chance to draft him. If he chose UCLA, the Lakers would be in the picture.

Also, there was the matter of salary. Wilt and whatever team that claimed and drafted him had to negotiate a mutually agreeable contract. As Gottlieb was to find, such negotiations would not be easy.

By the time Wilt was a high school senior, he stood 7 feet tall, perhaps a shade more. He would not allow himself to be measured. He weighed 230 pounds.

The best estimates are he stopped growing when he was 17.

This story has been told but it's worth repeating. As a high school youngster, Wilt would be waiting at a bus stop or enjoying a cup of coffee in a restaurant and a stranger would come up to him and say, "Excuse me, but . . ." Before the question could be framed, Wilt would answer, "Seven feet."

Yet Wilt was learning to endure the gawkers. The popularity and recognition he had won as a basketball player made him believe that his exorbitant height wasn't so bad after all.

Though Wilt, as a freshman high school student, was often shy and easily embarrassed, by the time he reached his high school senior year he was an assured young man. Basketball, and the eminence Wilt achieved in the sport, deserve much of the credit.

Wilt attained great popularity at Overbrook. His teammates as well as the fans would cheer him on during the games and clamor for him to score. They were proud to be on the same team with him.

But Wilt's future constantly intruded upon his present. Already the Philadelphia Warriors had manuevered to lay claim to him. During his last two years at Overbrook, the decision as to what college he would attend began to take on monumental proportions.

It seemed every college in the country wanted him and the competition for his services became as fierce as anything he had ever seen on a basketball court. Every day when he arrived home from school there would be letters awaiting him from colleges and his mother would tell him of the long distance calls that had come. Often there would be a college recruiter waiting in the living room to see him. Wilt did not let the general tumult or the excited promises of "We'll make it worth your while" bewilder him. Calmly, in May before his graduation, he made his decision.

5

Tall Man

IT WAS DURING the late 1930's that the tall man first came to be valued as a basketball player. The change came about despite the fact that the 1937–1938 college season saw the elimination of the center jump after every basket, a style of play in which height bestowed a distinct advantage.

With the advent of World War II, the tall man really came into his own. Selective service snatched away normal-size player candidates right and left, so coaches fell back upon whatever manpower was at hand. Invariably available was the draft-exempt tall man.

The tall man played in the pivot from where he could shoot and feed, and the fast break tumbled in value as a piece of offensive strategy. When World War II was ended, and players of normal size became available again, the style of the game did not revert to what it had been in pre-war days. It stayed—with some exceptions, of course—a big fellow's sport. Significantly, on everyone's college All American team for 1945–1946 were Bob Kurland of Oklahoma A & M, and George Mikan of DePauw. Kurland was 7 feet tall; Mikan was almost that.

Yet though he was valued, the tall player had a mighty poor image. He was considered slow and tangle-footed. Often tall men were called "goons," a word the dictionary defines as meaning "awkward" or "stupid."

By the time Wilt Chamberlain was ready for graduation from Overbrook High, the game of basketball was most assuredly in the hands of the Goliaths. To the college coach of the mid-1950's, a tall and well-coordinated player had a greater value than a new field house. Indeed, if the player were tall enough and well coordinated enough, he might attract enough fans to buy a new field house.

As a high school senior, Wilt was tall, all right, but just as important, he was no goon. Therein lay his great value.

He could run, dribble, jump and pass smartly out of the pivot. He could spin and fade. He could hit with jumpers, one-handers from the corner and—if pressed —two-handers from the outside. He loved the game; he loved to win.

Among the nation's colleges there was a frightful crush to get him. It began long before his graduation from Overbrook. As early as 1953, when Wilt was 16 and a sophomore, the first approaches were made.

It was not only the colleges. There were professional teams in the National Basketball Association who would have taken him as soon as he received his high school diploma, without any college basketball experience at all. One source said Wilt could have commanded a $12,000 contract as a pro.

The Harlem Globetrotters, in the person of their major-domo, Abe Saperstein, wanted Wilt. But he turned his back on the pro feelers and gave Mr. Saperstein a polite "no, thank you." More than playing for pay, Wilt wanted an education.

By the time Wilt was a high school junior, he could count close to 100 colleges that had contacted him. The Philadelphia colleges made the first overtures, and for a time it seemed that La Salle had the inside track. Jackie Moore, an idol of Wilt's who had preceded him at Overbrook High, was a former La Salle player and it was thought he might influence Wilt's decision.

In addition, the La Salle team, thanks mainly to the superlative skills of Tom Gola, had achieved a fine national reputation. Gola was soon to graduate and Wilt, by taking his place, could achieve instant coast-to-coast eminence.

In his senior year, the competition became frantic. Before he graduated from high school, slightly more than 200 colleges had contacted him.

For *Look* Magazine, Wilt described them as "77 major schools" and "125 minor schools." Those classed major included just about every big basketball school in the country. "About the only place I didn't hear from was Alaska," says Wilt.

It is difficult to imagine the great pressure this harangue placed upon young Chamberlain.

Sometimes the coaches would make a direct approach, sometimes it would be an alumnus or a friend of the college, but during Wilt's last two years in high school, he could not answer the doorbell, pick up a telephone or leave his home without encountering some type of salesmanship on behalf of one college or another. "I was hounded," Wilt says. "They gave me no rest."

Almost every weekend following his junior year, Wilt would visit a different college campus, taking advantage of the expense-free flying trips colleges offered him. Often on Friday evening he would be picked up at home, flown to the university, be shown about and be returned late on Sunday. Usually he would stay at the home of a prominent alumnus.

Wilt inspected Oregon, Dayton, Denver, Cincinnati, Illinois, Michigan, Michigan State, Northwestern, Iowa, Indiana and Kansas. He made three trips to Kansas.

The inducements the colleges offered Wilt were largely the same. Basic was the cost-of-living scholarship. Just as the phrase implies, this included tuition, room, board and books. Most conferences also permitted their colleges to offer a small monthly fee—pocket money—though in some cases Wilt would have had to perform some campus job like waiting on table to merit this.

There are, of course, stringent regulations set down by the National Collegiate Athletic Association concerning what athletes can and cannot receive for their services. However, Wilt said some colleges hinted they would raise the ante if he were to choose them.

One school indicated that a campus job for Wilt's father was a possibility. Another offered to find a job and a suitable home nearby the campus for his sister, who tutored Wilt in his schoolwork. Other schools suggested they would guarantee him a cash bonus or a well-paying job after graduation. But Wilt says such offers were few and they were presented in a "cagey" way.

Wilt appraised the college offers calmly. His parents gave suggestions, and so did friends and relatives, but everyone realized the decision was going to be Wilt's and Wilt's alone.

The college Wilt planned to choose had to satisfy certain guidelines he had set. First of all, he wanted to attend a large university and one with a well-established basketball program. Second, he did not want to play in the East; he wanted to see what life was like away from the big cities.

Because he is a Negro, the South held no appeal to
him. An alumnus of a university that shall be unnamed
approached Wilt at an airline terminal one day and
tried to sell him on his alma mater. "We've never had
a Negro basketball player," his argument ran. "You
can be the first." Wilt replied he thought it would be
nice if someone else were first; he told the alumnus he'd
rather be second.

Wilt didn't seriously consider any schools on the
West Coast because he felt they played an inferior
brand of basketball. Later he admitted he was wrong
about that.

At length, Wilt sifted the college offers down to just
four. The finalists were Dayton, Michigan, Indiana
and Kansas. Dayton fell by the wayside when Wilt
encountered a "segregation thing" in the Ohio city. A
Dayton hotel refused him meal service in their dining
room.

By the spring of 1955 only Indiana and Kansas were
left. Kansas, of course, won.

There are few American universities as rich in basketball tradition as Kansas. For 40 years the Jayhawk
campus boasted the presence of the "inventor" of basketball, Dr. James Naismith. It was he who, in 1891,
hung two peach baskets on a gymnasium balcony at the
YMCA Training School in Springfield, Massachusetts
(now Springfield College), to provide a game for athletes bored with the routine of calisthenics.

Dr. Naismith earned his degree as Doctor of Medicine in Denver, and in 1898 he arrived at the University
of Kansas where he soon became Director of Athlet-
ics. Naturally, he brought the sport of basketball with
him, and the Jayhawks played their first schedule in the
winter of 1898–1899.

Dr. Naismith did not look upon basketball as we do
today. Humble and idealistic, he felt the game should
be played purely for recreation and for the improve-

ment of the participant's physical condition. To Dr. Naismith, the factor of competition was strictly secondary.

He never became an avid fan of Jayhawk basketball teams, and those who knew him reported he preferred to watch fencing and tumbling in preference to the game he created. Dr. Naismith died at his home in Lawrence, Kansas, on November 28, 1939.

In Dr. Naismith's early years at Kansas, a young player named Forrest "Phog" Allen came under his direction. Allen was a basketball demon. He played forward, center or guard, and he was elected team captain in 1907. A half a century later, when Wilt Chamberlain came upon the scene, Phog Allen was the Jayhawk coach and he had been for 39 stormy years.

For decades Allen ranked as one of basketball's most pre-eminent figures. Not only had he built a sterling record for himself as a coach, but he was notable for his contributions to basketball in many other areas. For instance, it was Allen who was largely responsible for basketball becoming an Olympic sport.

Shrewd and aggressive, Allen mapped a grand strategy to bring Wilt to Kansas. Aiding him in his recruiting drive he had a dozen influential Kansans, many of them Negroes. One was Dowdal Davis, general manager of the Kansas City *Call*. A Kansas alumnus, it was Davis who arranged the University's first approach to Wilt.

Other prominent Negroes who urged Wilt to choose Kansas were Etta Motten, the noted concert singer, and Lloyd Kerford, an affluent Kansas industrialist. The latter visited Wilt's parents and he entertained Wilt at his home in Atchinson, Kansas.

Prominent university alumni wrote letters to Wilt and his family praising the college. Sometimes they telephoned him or visited him at his home. Allen also called upon Chamberlain's mother to stress the fine education Wilt would receive if he decided to become a Jayhawk.

Cecil Mosenson, Wilt's high school coach, recalls that it was Phog Allen himself who was the key factor. "He was a tremendous salesman," Mosenson says. "On one trip to Kansas he had a whole reception committee waiting to greet us."

There was probably some personal motivation in Allen's great desire to net Wilt. The "old recruiter," as some newspapers called him, had reached the compulsory retirement age of 70, but he had no desire to leave his coaching post. Many observers speculated he felt he would be able to stay on as basketball mentor if he brought Wilt in.

On one of his excursions to Kansas, Wilt met Dr. Franklin D. Murphy, Chancellor of the University. He told Wilt that Kansas would give him a full scholarship —board, room and tuition—and would see to it that he received $15 a month to pay for his laundry and such. But Wilt would have to earn the $15 by selling programs at football games or performing some other campus job.

Believe it or not, that was all Wilt ever received from the University of Kansas.

In the weeks that followed the announcement that Wilt planned to attend Kansas, neither he nor the University officials were prepared for the great hue and cry raised. The outpouring of distortions and varnished truths was astonishing.

The editor of a newspaper syndicate asked, "Why does a Philadelphia boy travel halfway across the country to attend college?"

A New York sports editor queried, "Isn't the NCAA investigating reports of a special fund that is due to mature on Wilt the Stilt's graduation?"

A sports writer cracked, "I feel sorry for Wilt Chamberlain. When he enters the NBA four seasons from now, he'll have to take a cut in salary."

An official at the University of Indiana announced, "We couldn't afford that boy. He was just too rich for our blood."

The gossip had it that Wilt had turned down all kinds of lavish offers to go to Kansas, and the incentive to do this had been a fat under-the-table bonus bestowed upon him by wealthy alumni. The rumor was that the money was being held in escrow for Wilt until he graduated. Depending upon the source, the amount varied from $10,000 to $25,000.

Walter Brown, President of the Boston Celtics, suddenly developed as one of Wilt's antagonists. Said Brown: "I have no definite proof what might be the figure, but it is a matter of fact that no one in the NBA can afford to pay Chamberlain what he gets at Kansas." At the time Brown made his statement, Boston's Bob Cousy, with an estimated salary of $22,000 a year, was the highest paid player in the league.

Brown declared that the NBA "should take steps immediately to keep him from playing."

Brown's words came as a rude shock to Wilt. He could hardly believe his ears.

Dick Harp, who had replaced Allen as Kansas coach, said that Brown's statements were "too ridiculous to dignify by comment." Eddie Gottlieb's reply took the same tack.

The situation was a bad one and it embittered Wilt.

Then the National Collegiate Association of America got into the act, and in their effort to find athletic code violations, they made the bad situation worse. Nowadays Wilt calls the NCAA "a real ring-a-ding outfit." His impression of the organization was formed during these college days and even before.

Wilt's first contact with the NCAA came when he was a high school senior. Officials of the organization wanted to know what college he planned to attend and the reasons why.

Then as a student at Kansas, they summoned him to

their headquarters in Kansas City, and put him through an exhausting four-hour question and answer session which they tape-recorded. Wilt answered the questions wholly and civilly, and when the session was over the chief interrogator told him, "It was nice talking to you but I don't believe a word of it."

Most of the questions concerned Wilt's 1956 Oldsmobile convertible. He explained to the NCAA that cars were always a sort of hobby with him. In 1953 he bought a 1949 Oldsmobile for about $700, money that he had saved by working summers as a "borscht bellhop," as he termed the job, at Kutshers, a resort in the Catskill Mountains of New York.

The following year—1954—he bought a 1951 Buick for $600 and the Oldsmobile. Then in 1956, he purchased a 1953 Oldsmobile for $900 and the Buick. The 1953 Olds was the car he brought to Kansas with him.

During his sophomore year at Kansas, Wilt spotted a year-old Cadillac he wanted. The dealer wouldn't take Wilt's Oldsmobile in partial payment, so Wilt had a local used car dealer sell the Oldsmobile for him. It brought about $900. The balance of the Cadillac's cost —$1,500—Wilt had to finance. The dealer took his notes.

In 1960, two years after Wilt had left college and was playing professional basketball for the Philadelphia Warriors, the NCAA announced that Kansas was being put on a two-year athletic probation. And the principal charge leveled against the university was that Wilt's Cadillac had been a gift to him from Kansas boosters. Representatives of "athletic interests" of the University had put up $1,564 for the car's purchase, the NCAA said.

6

Jayhawk

"KANSAS WAS GREAT," Wilt says. "I'll never regret the years I spent there."

Despite the gossip and the rumors that concerned his decision to attend the University of Kansas, Wilt looks back warmly upon his college career.

He was a popular student. He was dean of pledges in the Kappa Alpha Psi fraternity. He roomed in the modern Carruth-O'Leary Dormitory with track star Charley Tidwell, and a special 7 foot 6 inch bed was built for him. The room came to be a gathering place for Jayhawk players during breaks from class or after practice sessions.

Often Wilt and Charley would double-date, and dancing, movies or bowling would provide the entertainment.

Tidwell said in having Wilt as a roommate one source of friction never occurred. "My clothes were always in the closet," said the 5 feet 6 inch Tidwell. "Wilt wasn't the clothes-borrowing kind."

During his sophomore year, Wilt instituted a campus fad. During basketball practice sessions he took to wearing a black leather Ivy League cap. Soon each of his teammates was wearing one, and the next thing he knew a good percentage of the males on campus had blossomed out in the fashion.

Besides basketball, Wilt's interests included cars, the avocation that had so interested the NCAA, and music —rhythm and blues. He had a collection of 50 albums, and on road trips with the team he took along a selection of his discs and his record player.

Wilt's interest in popular music led him to become a disc jockey on the college radio station. Then, in his junior year, he broadcast a tape-recorded program on Station KLWN in Lawrence. The NCAA was to quiz him about this activity too, and about income he might have derived from it. But Wilt assured NCAA officials he received no pay; he did the program because he liked it.

Wilt chose the number 13 for his crimson and blue Jayhawk uniform. Actually, he wore numbers 12 *and* 13. Kansas followed the recommendations of the Big Seven Rules committee that odd numbers be worn on the road and even numbers at home. This was to prevent officials from being confused by two players wearing the same numbers and calling a foul on the wrong player. But how could any official ever confuse Wilt the Stilt with anyone else?

On each road trip, he was assigned a different roommate. In making reservations for the team, university authorities always requested a special bed for Wilt. If none was available, he had to make do in a standard double bed in which, as he expressed it, he would just "fold up a little."

The public's bulging stares bothered him less and less.

"Why should they?" he told Milt Gross of the New

York *Post* when Gross visited the Kansas campus. "My height is getting me an education and all the other things I want. It's not too bad having people know me."

Indeed, Wilt was becoming well known. There was constant newspaper publicity, and toward the end of his sophomore year, national magazines began to pay attention to him. Before Wilt had reached his twenty-first birthday, he had been the subject of feature articles in *Life, Look, Time* and *Newsweek*.

A publicity man was assigned to him on what amounted to a full time basis. And, in the manner of a Hollywood movie studio, the athletic department of the University had publicity pictures of Wilt printed by the hundreds. They were stamped with his autograph and sent out to fans who requested them.

Wilt majored in Business Administration and held a B average during his freshman and sophomore years. For his junior year, a local sportscaster named Marty Moore prevailed upon him to switch to a B.S. (Bachelor of Science) course, majoring in language.

In the classroom he usually sat in the front row, so he could stretch out his legs.

He regarded himself as "a pretty good student." Eventually, however, his marks fell below his usual standard. He never failed a subject, but in two courses he received D's. He blamed his preoccupation with basketball for his academic decline.

Wilt continued his interest in track and field. In the Big Eight Indoor Track Meet in 1958, Wilt cleared 6 feet 6¾ inches in the high jump, the best of his career, to tie with Joe Green of Missouri for first place. For a time he gave thought to entering the 1960 Olympic Games.

When Wilt made his court debut at Kansas, the whole world of basketball was watching.

It came early in his freshman year and, as has often

been the case when Wilt is thrust in the spotlight's glare, he responded with a performance touched with brilliance. The game itself was of little importance, merely the annual meeting of the freshman team and the Jayhawk Varsity. It usually attracted only the slightest interest, but the Chamberlain name in the freshman line-up stirred such excitement that on the night of the game a throng of 14,000 crammed their way into the giant University of Kansas field house.

The crowd came to roar at Wilt's every move, and what he did kept them in a frenzy.

He scored an astonishing 42 points and almost by himself led the freshman to an unprecedented 81–71 victory over the Jayhawk Varsity, and this was a varsity team that was favored to win the Big Seven (now the Big Eight) conference title.

Wilt, who complained he felt sick before the game, did not think his performance was quite up to par. "I couldn't seem to get rolling," he said afterward.

Nevertheless, what he accomplished won him praise from every quarter. Phog Allen, who celebrated his 70th birthday on the night of the game, declared: "Wilt could team with two Phi Beta Kappas and two co-eds and give us a battle."

An era of wild success was predicted for the Jayhawkers once Wilt became eligible for varsity play. To most observers, Wilt was not 7 feet tall, he was at least twice that.

Yet for the rest of his freshman year, Wilt slipped into relative obscurity. Under Big Seven rules, freshmen were not allowed to play a formal schedule. Instead, they scrimmaged among themselves or against the varsity under the eye of freshman coach Dick Harp, a longtime assistant to Allen.

Allen had a separate gym for practice sessions and in the gym he had had 12-foot baskets mounted. (In college basketball and also in professional play, baskets are placed 10 feet from the floor.) In scrimmages, Wilt would hit the rim of the 12-foot hoop, and sometimes his hand went over it.

Often Allen would attend a freshman practice to observe how his spindly charge was progressing. One of the coach's ambitions was to take the line drive character out of Wilt's shots, but he was only mildly successful. Allen also had Wilt work to improve his defensive effectiveness.

Wilt's sophomore year at the University of Kansas got off on a jarring note, for Phog Allen's bid to extend his service beyond his retirement age was denied. The coach protested loudly but to no avail. One source said Allen was taken from the field house kicking and screaming.

To replace Allen, Dick Harp was moved up to varsity status. Wilt liked the mild-mannered Harp but he liked Allen better, and he had looked forward with some eagerness in playing for him. His retirement vexed Wilt.

Jayhawk fans got another quick look at Wilt in the annual freshman-varsity meeting in November. Wilt this time, of course, represented the varsity.

Playing only 15 minutes, he tossed in 18 points and put on a sparkling defensive show. The outcome of the game wasn't in doubt for a single second, and the varsity won by a lopsided 87–40 count. Kansas boosters went home that night talking about a national championship.

A few weeks later, another stunning Chamberlain performance increased such talk. It was Wilt's varsity debut and a crowd of more than 15,000 jammed into the Kansas field house to watch.

Against a solid Northwestern team, Wilt scored the Jayhawks' first 11 points, propelling the team to a fast 11–2 advantage. From that plateau he went on to shatter every game scoring and rebound record in

Kansas' history. He netted 52 points in total, and defensively he was almost as spectacular. He controlled both boards and gathered in 31 rebounds. The final score saw Kansas on top, 87–69.

A new flood tide of publicity came on the heels of Wilt's latest triumph. Everywhere the Jayhawks were instantly acclaimed as the No. 1 basketball power in the country. Indeed, a few days after the game, Kansas found itself perched at the very top of the first Association Press sportscasters' poll of the season.

Unfortunately, Wilt's pre-eminence had not escaped basketball's rulemakers. During his sophomore year at Kansas the long history of legislative flim-flam began, some of which had been meant to put a check on Chamberlain's skills.

One new rule specified a player shooting a foul was not allowed to cross the foul line until the ball struck the rim or the backboard. Wilt had developed the habit of shooting fouls off a springing jump, an exercise that brought him to the basket about the same time as the ball. Another new rule, and another for which Wilt was indirectly responsible, prohibited a player from guiding a teammate's shot into the basket.

The rules now also prevented a player from making an out-of-bounds toss in *over* the backboard. This strategy, a favorite of Bill Russell's when he was starring for the University of San Francisco, made easy tap-ins possible for very tall players.

The new rules did very little to hamper Wilt, however. He ripped through the opposition like a prairie cyclone, and Kansas victory piled upon victory.

Bill Strannigan, coach of Iowa State University, saw Wilt in action in a game against Marquette. "I'd enjoy the next few weeks a lot more if I hadn't seen him," said Strannigan, whose team had an upcoming date with the Jayhawks. "He's the greatest player I've ever seen.

"Why, once he even led a fast break. He was the middle man, and he passed off behind his back to set-up the score. Who ever heard of a 7 foot player doing that? He's unbelievable."

"What can be done about him?" someone asked.

"Just be patient and he'll graduate," Strannigan replied.

Frank McGuire, coach of the University of North Carolina, wisecracked about Wilt's presence on the scene. "I told Phog he would be killing basketball by bringing that boy into school. Some night Chamberlain is going to score 130 points and the other coach will lose his job."

Jack Ramsey of St. Joseph's College in Philadelphia lauded Wilt for his value on defense. "He's a tremendous psychological factor defensively," said Ramsey. "His opponents shoot with one eye on the basket and one on Wilt."

In the annual Big Seven holiday tournament Wilt lived up to everything that was being said about him. He smashed all tourney scoring records. Often he would set himself under his own board and call out to a teammate to shoot, perfectly confident in his ability to retrieve the ball if the shot wasn't good. Naturally, Kansas won the tournament.

Yet coaches who were unfortunate enough to have the University of Kansas on their schedule did not give up hope of somehow shackling big Wilt. Through sleepless nights they plotted defenses against him, and in team practice sessions they drilled upon strategies that would keep Chamberlain's point production within reasonable limits. No one thought it was possible to stop him entirely.

After Kansas' first varsity game, in which Wilt scored 52 points, there were never less than two men guarding him. In fact, two men were rather the exception. Most often there were three men; sometimes four.

Two of the chief plotters against Wilt and his fellow Jayhawks were Iowa State's Bill Strannigan and his assistant, Bob Lamson. Their team lost to Kansas in the Big Seven holiday tourney, but the pair had a plan how Wilt might be subdued and the Jayhawks stopped.

Under their design, Iowa's 6 feet 9 inch center, Don Medsker, would play in front of Chamberlain to grab or block passes fired into him. The Iowa forwards were instructed to sag off in back of Wilt with the same motives. Iowa's guards were to be used to harass Kansas' outside shooters.

Of course, this system permitted the Jayhawks some unguarded shots, particularly from the corners, but Strannigan figured many of these would go beyond Chamberlain's reach since they would not be deflected by the backboard.

The Iowa coaches also set a ball control strategy which dictated the team was to hold possession until a man was worked free for an unbothered shot.

The teams met before a wild and shrieking partisan crowd at the Ames (Iowa) Field House, and Strannigan's master plan worked as he had prayed it would. For the first time that season the Jayhawks were sent down to defeat. From that night on, they were never again regarded as supernatural.

The Iowa plan worked to such perfection that Wilt did not score a field goal in the first half. All told, he netted only five of them and seven free throws, though two of these came in the last nine seconds of play to tie the score. Don Medsker fired a jump shot from 15 feet at the final buzzer to give Iowa the edge, 39–37.

Two weeks later, at Kansas, the Jayhawks paid back the injury as Wilt thwarted Strannigan's battle plan by sliding off his post position, and opening up shooting room underneath for his teammates. Wilt plucked 24 rebounds—more than twice as many as any other Jayhawk. Dick Harp called the game Kansas' finest of the year.

The earlier defeat at the hands of Iowa State was the only one the Jayhawks suffered in Big Seven play, and they won their conference title with considerable ease. But no one was conceding them the national championship. There were too many other good teams.

There was Frank McGuire's North Carolina Tar Heels, undefeated in 24 games. They were a tall team and a fast one. There was the University of California, which harassed the opposition to death with its pressing man-to-man defense. There was San Francisco, national college champions over the two previous years, but now without Bill Russell who had graduated. There was SMU, Kentucky and Michigan.

All of these and some others were to clash in the NCAA tournament and out of it very likely would come the team that would be acclaimed the nation's best.

In the Western Regional playoffs, Kansas first defeated SMU. It was a nerve-tingling game from the opening tip, but the outcome was signaled when SMU's fine center, Jim Krebs, fouled out with more than a full quarter remaining. The following night the Jayhawks faced Oklahoma City University and overpowered them with a mighty second half spurt.

Both games were played in Dallas, and on the first night Wilt took an enormous amount of booing and hooting from the partisan fans. He never lost his poise, however, a fact which seemed to heighten the intensity of the abuse.

The fans were further infuriated by SMU's defeat, and they returned the next evening for the Oklahoma City University game in a still angrier mood.

It was a rough evening for Wilt. Everytime he made a move shouts of "Foul! Foul!" would come from the crowd. They threw seat cushions and coins—mostly pennies—out on to the court. They called Wilt names.

A few days after the contest, referee Al Lightner said that to him it seemed Oklahoma City players were "deliberately dumping Chamberlain and Negro guard Maurice King. The trouble seemed to be," said Lightner, "that they were dark-skinned." All in all, it was an ugly incident.

For the tournament finals and semi-finals, played at the Kansas City Municipal Auditorium, the Jayhawks got back to concentrating on basketball. The semi-finals matched four teams: Kansas vs. San Francisco and North Carolina vs. Michigan.

Kansas and Wilt were brilliant against the San Franciscans. Surprisingly, they out-defensed them. And they shot with an amazing 59.6 average. The final score saw the Jayhawks on top, 80–56.

In a triple overtime thriller, North Carolina overcame Michigan, 74–70.

So the season came down to a final game: Kansas vs. North Carolina.

The Tar Heels had big and mobile men that made a victory over Kansas very much of a possibility. They had 6 feet 5 inch Lennie Rosenbluth, who featured an excellent variety of shots. They had Tommy Kearns, a sizzling playmaker. They had Joe Quigg, a 6 feet 9 inch pivot man. The Tar Heels also had experience and poise, and poise was a much needed commodity when dealing with Kansas. Many times that year teams had been menaced into defeat by Wilt's presence on the court.

North Carolina also had the shrewd Frank McGuire as their coach. McGuire schemed carefully for this one.

McGuire's philosophy regarding Wilt was not entirely new. "Chamberlain is like every other player," he said. "He cannot score unless he gets his hands on the ball. What you've got to do is keep the ball away from him. You must cut down on the number of shots he takes."

McGuire's examination of the situation went further. "Wilt is the most dangerous *after* he has made his shot," the North Carolina coach observed. "That's when he moves in to dunk. That's when you've got to stop him."

From the opening minute, McGuire's charges displayed wonderful self-assurance, and throughout the game they remained as cool as watermelons in a Carolina field.

They brought the ball up the court with the greatest deliberation, then suddenly they would break a man free with a quick move or a sharp pass. If the man did not believe he was sufficiently clear to score, he would whip the ball back into play. In the first ten minutes of the game, the Carolinians did not miss a single shot.

Meanwhile Wilt was having formidable problems. On defense, two Tar Heels—Rosenbluth in front and Quigg in back—pinched him in. "He was mashed like a frankfurter in a roll," Dick Harp said.

Rosenbluth's job was to prevent the ball from getting to Wilt. Quigg worked to keep Chamberlain from moving in under the board. The two had the height and the experience to be effective in their roles. The three other Tar Heels defensed against the rest of the Jayhawks.

This defense would have come apart at the seams had the Jayhawks been able to hit from the outside, but they were sad in this respect. Halftime statistics showed Kansas with a dismal 27.3 shooting percentage, while North Carolina had a sizzling 64.7 average and—naturally—the lead, 29–22.

The second half looked like a taped replay of the first. Kansas was a bit more accurate and North Carolina a bit less, but the differences weren't enough to sway the course of the game.

Since the Jayhawks could not hit with any degree of

consistency from the outside, they tried to work the ball in to Wilt. But when they got it to him, he had all he could do to shoot. The Tar Heels played him so close they were standing on his insteps. Seldom could he take the step he needed to launch his shot.

Through the pressure packed game, Wilt attempted only 15 field goals. He made six of them.

Late in the second half Rosenbluth, who had played a standout game on offense, fouled out. The game ended in a 46–46 tie and three overtime periods were needed to settle the match.

Each of the overtime sessions was a tingler. In the first one, each team scored two points. In the second, neither team could score.

In the third overtime period, the score was tied three times and then Kansas edged ahead, 53–52.

Only six seconds remained. Then someone fouled Joe Quigg. He sank both free throws. Kansas had lost.

It was a bitter defeat for Wilt. He scored "only" 23 points, well below his season game average of close to 30. The fact that he was voted the tournament's Most Valuable Player did very little to ease his discontent.

It was not only losing that upset him. It was the way the team lost. Being crowded in so he could not move was a frustrating way to play the game. The stubborn ball control patterns that opponents worked against the Jayhawks didn't sit well with him either. "That's not basketball," he protested. Many times over the season Wilt had been disenchanted with the college brand of court play. Kansas' loss to Frank McGuire and the Tar Heels worked to increase his disenchantment.

7

The Author

THERE WAS NO "next year" for the Jayhawks.

The following season the Kansas team could achieve no more than a cheerless 18–5 record and they failed to qualify for the NCAA Tournament. For Wilt it was a season pocked with many low points.

The fact that he was acclaimed as a college All-America for the second consecutive year did little to brighten him or his followers. After all, everyone expected it.

It was a rough season. Many times Wilt was painfully hurt by opposition elbows and knees.

Sometimes, when he would leap high for a rebound, a small player would run underneath and trip him up as he came down. He took some bad falls.

And more and more the tactical side of the game displeased him.

Typical was an early season game in which the Kansans faced St. Joseph's College. It was played at the Palestra in Philadelphia and sold out days in advance for it marked the first time Wilt was to play in his home city since his Overbrook days almost three years before.

The Jayhawks won the match, but Wilt's fans were keenly disappointed by what they saw.

Offensively Kansas had only one pattern of play. It worked like this: Wilt, usually, would clear the boards and the Jayhawks would bring the ball up the court, waiting for Wilt to get into position before a shot was taken.

Then Wilt would anchor himself in the pivot ("like the Statue of Liberty," said Jack Ryan of the Philadelphia *Bulletin*), his hands high, waving for a pass. Of course, he would be pinched in by two or three defensive men.

Eventually the ball would be worked into Wilt, and he would take the shot or pass back. If someone else shot, he would rebound.

Very seldom was there any variation in this pattern. There was no give-and-go strategy, few screens and few picks. Wilt's followers lamented that the big fellow's talents were being dissipated.

To Wilt, too, this brand of ball was discouraging. He preferred to move. He preferred to vary the play.

Wilt now began to relish the time he could play as a professional. Under the pro rules, the zone defense, which so cluttered up the lanes, was not allowed. The pros had to employ a man-to-man defense, and Wilt felt this would prevent players from sagging off on him. At least he hoped it would.

Sometimes, to keep Wilt from getting the ball, teams would freeze it for long periods of time. Someone counted up, and Oklahoma State, in a game against the Jayhawks, had once passed the ball 160 times before taking their shot. Wilt felt that this was absolutely ridiculous. It made the game a burlesque of what it should be. But under the pro rules, such inane strategy would be ruled out by the 24-second clock, which forced teams to shoot within that time.

Because of these assorted offensive and defensive absurdities, Wilt felt he was no longer sharpening his skills at Kansas. He began to doubt seriously whether he would ever be able to compete with the likes of Bill Sharman, Bill Russell and Bob Pettit.

However, Wilt still had more than a year to wait before he would be eligible for competition in the National Basketball Association. The draft rights to him belonged to the Philadelphia Warriors, and they, of course, planned to exercise these rights. But under the NBA rules, even though drafted, he would not become eligible to play until the year his college class graduated.

Toward the end of Wilt's sophomore year, rumors began to be heard that he was planning to quit Kansas. Wilt denied the talk. So did the University.

As Wilt's junior year at Kansas drew to a close, the rumors became louder and more persistent.

Significantly, they reached the ears of one I. R. ("Iggy") McVay, a large, ruddy, gray-haired gentleman on the staff of *Look* Magazine.

Late in March of his junior year, Wilt decided to attend the NBA championship playoffs between Boston and St. Louis. There McVay spotted him. He asked Wilt if there were any truth to the stories that he was planning to leave Kansas. Wilt shrugged.

"Well," said McVay, "if you have anything to say, get in touch with me." And he left Wilt his phone number.

Indeed, Wilt did have something to say. And for the money *Look* offered to pay him, he was willing to say it to them exclusively. He called McVay.

As a result of the call and the negotiations that followed, the issue of *Look* for June 10, 1958, featured an article bylined by Wilt and it was titled, "Why I am Quitting College."

It began:

> I'm quitting college and will not go back to the University of Kansas this fall.
>
> I have sound reasons for leaving Kansas and college sports, even though I have a season's eligibility remaining and a year to go for my degree. I am arranging a big barnstorming tour, which will give me a chance to play some real basketball for a change. The game I was forced to play at K.U. wasn't basketball. It was hurting my chances of ever developing into a successful professional player.
>
> The barnstorming tour will also give me a chance to make some money. I need money to help my family. There are nine of us, six boys and three girls, and we've always had to struggle to get along. My father, 57, still has to work as a handyman for $60 a week. My mother, 56, still has to go out as a domestic. I want to fix it up so they can stop working and enjoy life more. The only way I could ever help them is through the dollar value of my basketball ability.

The article was only Part I of Wilt's literary endeavor for *Look*. Part II was contracted for at the same time, though it was neither written nor scheduled for publication until the completion of Wilt's first season as a professional.

The barnstorming tour that Wilt spoke of, to be a 160 game junket between two 10-man squads, one of Negroes, one of whites, never became a reality.

Instead, Wilt had another surprise. In mid-summer of 1958, he suddenly announced that he was joining the most bizarre of all basketball teams, the famous Harlem Globetrotters.

8

Globetrotter

ABE SAPERSTEIN was a pear-shaped little man with king-size basketball ideas. In the winter of 1927, he took five Negro players, a battered Model-T he bought from a funeral director and a fair amount of *chutzpeh* and he set out on the road. They played their first game on a bitter cold night in Hinckley, Illinois, and earned $75. That was the beginning for the Harlem Globetrotters, a team that was to become one of the most astonishing court attractions of all time.

The Globetrotters didn't start making much more than hot dog money until 1940. Before that, days were so lean that Saperstein doubled as a ball boy, chauffeur and even as a team substitute.

Real success came after World War II. The Trotters' blend of clever basketball and brilliant showmanship lured sellout crowds into basketball arenas across the country. In 1953 in the Los Angeles Memorial Coliseum, they shattered the one-day attendance mark for basketball when 36,256 fans watched them play the College All Stars in afternoon and night contests. The team was in such demand Saperstein split it into two touring squads and the portly 5 feet 5 inch owner began to describe himself as, "The man who found the golden basket."

In 1952, to celebrate the twenty-fifth anniversary of the team, Saperstein scheduled the Globetrotters on the first world tour in the history of basketball. More success. In England, Western Europe, Africa, the Near East and the Far East, fans flocked to see them. In the years that followed, the team played in some 87 countries in all, and before personalities as diverse as Pope Pius XII and Russia's Khrushchev.

"Laugh standards are the same all over the world," Saperstein once said in explaining the team's success. "Wars, depressions and one crisis after another are commonplace everywhere. Our fans are looking for escape from worry and tension when they come to see us play and we never want to fail them."

It has often been said that the Trotters' great lure was their refusal to take themselves seriously. With their tricks and tomfoolery, they gave the impression that they played the game with one purpose—to entertain.

Saperstein was intent upon making Wilt a member of the Trotters for good reason. The troupe lacked a personality, a real drawing card. The Trotters had once featured two stars: Goose Tatum, a comic sensation, and Marques Haynes, a fantastic dribbler, but the pair had deserted Saperstein to form a competing team. Their replacements never achieved the great popularity that they had been able to claim. Saperstein was willing to pay well for a "name."

For signing with the Globetrotters in July 1958 for nine months of toil, Wilt received a sum estimated to be between $45,000 and $65,000. It probably tended toward the lower figure. Though the precise amount has never been revealed, one thing is certain: it was the largest sum ever paid to a college basketball star to turn professional.

One of the first things Wilt did after signing with Saperstein was to purchase for his parents a handsome ranch-type house on Cobbs Creek Parkway in a placid suburban area of Philadelphia. Wilt has always been generous with his family. The new home was characteristic of this.

It must be said that Wilt's signing with the Globetrotters did not bring him complete joy. He was somewhat remorseful about leaving Kansas. He did indeed want to complete his education; his mother also wanted him to remain in college. But the alternative reasons were simply too alluring for him to stay.

Then, too, Wilt came in for some chiding for his decision to join Saperstein's razzle-dazzle outfit. Critics recalled one of the prime reasons he gave for leaving Kansas was because he wasn't able to further develop his basketball skills there. "I've always got three or four guys hanging on me," was the way he put it.

What his critics wanted to know was how Wilt expected to improve his talents while playing as a Globetrotter. "What's he going to learn?" one wanted to know. "How to kick the ball in the basket?"

However, Wilt was determined not to be a clown—at least not all the time. He and Saperstein decided it would be best if Wilt played guard. He thereby became the biggest backcourt man in the history of basketball.

Wilt played guard for very solid reasons. It gave him a chance to do a lot of things he had never done before. It enabled him to move more, to handle the ball more and to practice feints and the best angles for driving in.

Defensively, of course, he played under the basket and protected the man in the pivot. But on offense he practiced his outside shooting.

Playing as a member of the Globetrotters is hardly a recommended method to hone one's skills to professional sharpness—indeed, playing with an aggregation like the Trotters can lead to bad habits, such as walking or carelessness on defense—but in Wilt's case, it was not time wasted. He was serious-minded in his tenure with the team and while it did not serve to improve his artistry to any great degree, it certainly did him no harm.

By playing in the backcourt, Wilt added immensely to the Trotters' appeal. The usual routine was to feed the ball to Wilt near the center line. "In two steps he'd be at the basket dunking it," Saperstein said. "The people went nuts." Meadowlark Lemon, the most renowned of Saperstein's court jesters, held down his familiar role of the Trotters' gyrating pivot man.

On the evening of July 14, Wilt joined the Globetrotters in Turin, Italy. Nobody knew the Dipper in Turin; perhaps only a handful in all of Italy, yet he was an immediate sensation. After watching him dunk baskets at the local arena, the people of Turin became enchanted with him. On the local streets, crowds followed him about as if he were a tour director.

In Milan, he borrowed a bicycle from a youngster and rode off. An hour later when he returned to the hotel, a string of 30 bikes was following him.

The European tour that year was not altogether profitable for the Trotters. There were riots in France, a bus strike in London and almost always abominable weather.

The team had to cancel a game in Naples because Italia Air Lines was grounded by a 48 hour strike.

At Cortina D'Ampezo, site of the 1964 Winter

Olympics, the court was laid over the ice skating rink. Boys on skates recovered loose balls and throughout the game rain poured down. To Wilt, Haddington Center seemed at least a million miles away.

Vienna was a high point. There the Globetrotters opened a brand new sports arena, and standing-room-only crowds watched Saperstein's court wizards.

Later in the year, the team returned to the United States.

In mid-October the Globetrotters were scheduled into Madison Square Garden, and Wilt's first appearance on the most famous of all basketball courts excited New York City's curiosity. The newspapers even covered Globetrotter practice sessions and the usually blasé New York writers raved about Wilt's coordination and his shooting skill. The photographers got Wilt and Ray Felix, the New York Knickerbockers' 6 feet 11 inch center, to stand back to back to show there *was* someone taller than Felix.

The Knicks were engaged in pre-season practice scrimmage when the Trotters came out onto the floor for their workout. Most of the Knicks had never seen Wilt before. Their praise was enthusiastic.

"He's not skinny; he's built," said one.

"Look how he moves," said another. "He's not awkward at all."

The game, which saw the Globetrotters face their perennial patsys, the College All Stars, was a tremendous sellout. "We could have filled Yankee Stadium," said one Garden official.

Wilt entertained the huge crowd with a dazzling exhibition. He didn't do much shooting; he didn't do much rebounding, but the way he handled the ball and more important, the way he moved with wonderful quick and fluid speed, won him glowing praise. "He's great," was the consensus.

Did the Trotters win? The Trotters always win. For the 1958–1959 season, the Globetrotters' record—for both touring squads—was 411–0. Not bad.

After New York City, the Globetrotter tour settled into its routine, and "routine" with the Trotters is no picnic. It is a long series of one night stands. It is eating on the run, and hot dogs or hamburgers and acrid coffee in paper cups are featured on one's diet. It is riding in buses, hour after endless hour.

And when you are 7 feet $\frac{1}{16}$ of an inch tall, the grind is much more fatiguing than it is for a person of less spectacular dimensions. The bus seats are never big enough; all beds are too small.

Never—for anyone—is there enough time to sleep. It is a wearing, wearying business.

Wilt was in constant demand to go on television and meet with the press in cities where the team played. Often that meant he had to get into town before the rest of the players. But Saperstein lauded him. "He never shirked it," he said.

At Christmas time Wilt was given a week's vacation from the rigors of the tour, while the other members of the troupe junketed to Alaska for a series of appearances for the U. S. Department of State.

In April, when Wilt's contract expired, Saperstein could look back upon a season of fine success. He judged business to be up about 20 percent over the previous season.

Wilt had one last fling with the Trotters before he joined the pros. In July, Abe Saperstein cabled Wilt from Russia and asked him to join the Globetrotters there. "Saperstein needs me," Wilt told a friend and as soon as he could he made plane reservations for Moscow.

The team stayed at the Ukraine Hotel in Moscow and played exhibitions—nine of them—at the Lenin Memorial Stadium. The first game (Saperstein brought along the College All Stars for opposition) was played exclusively for officials of the Communist Party who wanted to assay the Trotters' antics before allowing the local populace to witness the team. They decided there was nothing subversive about the dunk shot or the basketball drop kick and Moscovites were allowed to surge in.

In Red Square one day, quite unexpectedly, the team met the highest of high Russian officials and Wilt got to shake hands with Khrushchev.

As a Globetrotter, Wilt admits, with a nostalgic smile, that he had "the greatest time of my life." Despite the rigors of schedule, it was something of a year-long frolic for him.

The time he spent as a Trotter worked very much to Wilt's benefit. He became stronger and faster and broadened out noticeably. His weight reached 250 pounds.

But it was more than that. To use an over-worked word, his "image" changed considerably. No longer was he thought of as just a college youngster. He had become a much more valued commodity.

The NBA, in general, and Eddie Gottlieb and the Warriors, in particular, were absolutely convinced now that Wilt would be not less than sensational. In league cities across the country *Standing Room Only* signs were getting a fresh coat of paint. But the situation was a bit different than it had been a year before, for now Saperstein wanted Wilt, too. And he was willing to pay him an even fancier salary than he had given him the first year.

Naturally, this play of events gave Wilt great bargaining power, and seasoned by two years of dealing with college recruiters in his pre-Kansas days, Wilt knew how to use the power to his advantage.

At the time the owners of the NBA had a $25,000 ceiling on players' salaries. Bob Cousy of the Boston

Celtics and Bob Pettit of the St. Louis Hawks were in that class.

But such was not for Wilt. Though a rookie, he wanted more than the top NBA stars were receiving.

He now ranked as the most publicized player of all time, college or professional. More important, he knew he did. Saperstein wanted him; Gottlieb, who had been waiting anxiously for more than four years, wanted him.

Through the early months of 1959, Wilt played it cool. When asked if he was planning on re-signing with the Trotters, he would smile and give a meaningless shrug.

Asked if he was joining the Warriors, he would shake his head and mumble, "I don't know."

"When will you know?" one interviewer persisted.

"I don't know," Wilt said.

It was all an astute bit of maneuvering, worthy of someone well beyond Wilt's 21 years.

At length Wilt signed with Gottlieb and the Warriors. The prestige of playing in the NBA and the opportunity to test his skills against players regarded as the best in the world were important factors in his decision. But so was money.

The salary Wilt earned as an NBA rookie has never been officially revealed. But he received more than Russell, more than Cousy and more than Pettit— maybe $35,000, maybe as much as $50,000—much, much more than anyone had ever received before.

9

Debut

"HE TOOK A PASS, backed into me and leaped high in the air as if he had been propelled off a launching pad. When I jumped—and I'm 6 feet 8—my hands reached over the rim, but there was Wilt looking down at me, and stuffing the ball into the basket. At the same time the Philadelphia public address system screamed, 'Another Dipper Dunk!' It was horrifying."

So spoke Dolf Schayes, the periennial professional All Star of the Syracuse Nationals after a confrontation with Wilt in an exhibition game. Other pre-season critiques of the big man were not quite so stirring, but they never failed fairly to burst with praise.

Fuzzy Levane, the coach of the New York Knicks, who coached Wilt in a benefit game for Cincinnati's Maurice Stokes (who had been stricken with a paralyzing brain disease), said this: "It scares me to think what he'll be like in another season or two. With experience he'll be absolutely fabulous because the raw material is certainly there."

Said Al Bianchi, a teammate of Schayes' at Syracuse: "Who needs him in the league? What's going to happen to us little guys? With him in there goaltending, we'll never be able to get a lay-up."

Indeed, by October, when the season was ready to open, so much had been said and written about Chamberlain and his vast skills, that fans of the Philadelphia Warriors were looking forward not just to a winning team, but to a national championship.

After all, weren't Wilt's magnificent skills going to revolutionize the game of basketball? How could they do less for the Warriors?

Yet realists knew it was not going to be that simple. The 1958–1959 season had been a dismal one for Philadelphia. Dissatisfied with their coach, Al Cervi, and his driving tactics, the team had finished dead last.

But now the Warriors had a new coach in lanky and lantern-jawed Neil Johnston, for many years a high scoring center for Philadelphia, but whose career had been cut short by a knee injury. Johnston had been in sympathy with the team's complaints during the previous seasons, so the players were expected to respond to his command.

Despite their cellar finish, the Warriors were not without some respectable players. There was Paul Arizin for one, judged by many to be basketball's foremost practitioner of the jump shot. He had scored at the rate of at least twenty points a game over the previous six seasons. Often over those years defenders had double-teamed Arizin, but with Wilt at center for the Warriors, such tactics would be rash, so Arizin's scoring output—he had averaged 26.4 points per game the season before—was expected to improve.

Philadelphia's other corner man was Woody Sauldsberry, a fine rebounder with a facile skill for popping one-handers from the outside. Joe Grabowski, a 10 year veteran of pro ball, was the swingman, relieving either Arizin or Sauldsberry.

In the backcourt the Warriors were rich in talent. They had Guy Rodgers, lightning fast and a sharp passer. He was, in fact, compared to Boston's Bob Cousy for the way in which he handled the ball. Warrior fans could hardly wait to see him teamed with Chamberlain.

At the other guard position was Tom Gola and he, like the Philadelphia forwards, was expected to become improved by Chamberlain's presence in the line-up. Gola's talent was in keeping enemy attackers under continual harassment. He could make seemingly impossible interceptions, and with Wilt under boards to backstop him, Gola was expected to play with more daring and thereby more success than ever before.

But there were troubles—serious ones. Critics of the Warriors were quick to point out their backcourt men, while wonderfully deft as ball handlers, lacked skill as outside shooters. Another failing was an absence of depth. The team's reserves seldom showed varsity skill.

Eddie Gottlieb, the Warriors' owner, was aware of these shortcomings. He also was canny enough to realize that his skyscraping center was going to be pushed, pulled, hacked and generally mauled by Philadelphia's opponents in an effort to cut him down to size. The Warriors were hardly a shoo-in for the title. It was going to be a very rugged season.

The biggest problem that confronted the Warriors— and every other team, for that matter—was the mighty Boston Celtics. The previous season the Celts had taken an early lead and held it to the end. Almost without effort they defeated the Minneapolis Lakers in the playoffs that decided the league championship. They seemed a team without a single weakness.

They boasted a devastating and marvelously balanced attack. They showed masterful defensive prowess, primarily on the talent of remarkable Bill Russell.

In Tom Heinsohn, the Celtics had a superb shooter. In Bob Cousy and Bill Sharman, the team had the best backcourt men in basketball. If Chamberlain and his Philadelphia teammates were going to be beaten, the odds favored the Celtics as the team that would turn the trick.

For the Warriors the season opened in New York City's Madison Square Garden, with the Knickerbockers furnishing the opposition. Wilt Chamberlain could not have made a bigger splash if he had jumped off the George Washington Bridge into the Hudson River.

The huge arena was jammed to capacity, and Chamberlain quickly became the hero to the huge throng and the fans cheered his every move.

"Right from the beginning I could see what it was going to be like," said Fuzzy Levane. "On one of the game's early plays, Wilt and Kenny Sears went for a ball near the basket. They both got their hands on it but Wilt jumped up and dunked it into the basket with both hands. Sears was still hanging onto the ball. I swear I thought Chamberlain was going to stuff Kenny into the basket, too."

Wilt's amazing rebounding created a special kind of havoc at the Garden that night. Up he would drive amidst a wild flurry of elbows, hips, arms and, on a number of occasions, fists to snatch the ball from the backboard.

The Knick's strategy was to try to keep Chamberlain away from the basket, so he would have to rely on his fall-away push in order to score. Quickly this scheme backfired. Time and again Wilt's great speed enabled him to elude Charlie Tyra or his substitute, Johnny Green, assigned to defend against him.

Wilt would spot an opening and with one incredibly

long stride arrive at the basket. Guy Rodgers would rifle a pass somewhere in Wilt's vicinity. Up Wilt's arm would stretch and his hand would grab it. Then he would feint, spin and, more often than not, score.

On defense he was scarcely less devastating. He blocked shots no ordinary player would even attempt to block. Once he faced three fast-breaking Knicks at the Warrior basket and prevented a goal. The crowd was unbelieving.

The statistics of Wilt's debut looked like this: He captured 28 rebounds. He hit on 17 of 20 field goal attempts. Nine of his 15 foul shots were good. This gave him 43 points in the Warriors 118–109 victory. It was a magnificent performance.

Wilt was well satisfied, and not just because the Warriors had won and he had led the way. Many of his field goals had come in jumpers, a type of shot that requires skill as well as size. "I hope I showed them that I can do something besides dunk the ball," he said.

Philadelphia and Boston lived up to the pre-season estimates and they quickly opened up daylight between themselves and the other teams in the Eastern Division. The Warriors streaked to three consecutive victories, while the Celtics went five games without being beaten. Then early in November the two undefeated teams met in the Boston Garden with the league lead riding on the contest's outcome.

The game was intensely anticipated, but not so much because it would serve to give some insight into which team was superior. Instead, the game was heralded as the greatest man-to-man clash in modern basketball. Wilt Chamberlain's height and scoring punch—he had been averaging 39.6 points per game—were to be tested against the brilliance of Bill Russell, regarded as the finest defensive player in the game, possibly in history.

Russell, a polished and experienced veteran, in his fourth year as a professional, was off to his best start as a pro. He had an average of 22.2 points a game, far over his usual figure, and he boasted a 25.3 average in rebounds, higher than any of his previous league leading marks.

Despite these credits, most observers gave Chamberlain a slight advantage. His height was the chief reason; he held a four inch edge over Russell. He also was some 40 pounds heavier and had somewhat of an advantage in strength and power.

The day of the game Wilt tried to appear unbothered by the fuss that had been aroused. He spent most of the afternoon dozing diagonally across a pair of beds in Boston's Hotel Lenox. He ate an early dinner, signed a few autographs outside the hotel and then took a cab to the Garden. Wilt knew the meeting with Russell represented another test he must pass before he could be stamped a solid professional. This caused him some mental strain, and he hoped the nervousness wouldn't show.

Seldom, not even in the championship playoffs, has professional basketball known such excitement. The Boston Garden was sold out weeks in advance, and whatever tickets were available were grabbed up by scalpers who hawked them at $20 a pair.

When the players arrived at the Garden, all but a few seats were already filled. Spectators ringed the court during the warm-ups and every eye was on big Wilt. Loud oohs and aahs greeted his spectacular dunks.

No sooner was the game underway then a forgotten star stole the show. His name? Bob Cousy. He fed, feinted, drove and shot in typical Cousy fashion. He grabbed control of proceedings right at the start, and propelled the Celtics to a quick 22-7 lead. The Bostonians were never headed after that and were on top at the end, 115-106.

As for the greatly acclaimed duel between Chamberlain and Russell, it was pretty much of a standoff. Russell scored 22 points; Wilt got 30 (but he took twice as many shots). Russell out rebounded Chamberlain, 35–38. From the free throw line, Russell was 8 for 8, while Chamberlain missed 6 of 12.

But Wilt learned. He got something of a shock early in the game when Russell blocked his finger tip fall-away, his favorite shot. Never—through high school, in YMCA play, in two seasons of varsity basketball at Kansas or in three previous pro games—had that happened before. Never!

"I don't think I was nervous," Chamberlain said in the dressing room after the game. "But I was tense. Russell didn't play me the way I expected him to at all. I thought he'd guard me tighter. But he played off me and moved in on my jumper." Generally, Wilt was disappointed with his performance.

But he shouldn't have been. He made an indelible impression and a very favorable one.

Bill Russell was high in praise of Wilt. "I've played against men as big," he said. "But never against any one that good *and* big. You can't relax for a second against him.

"He's the best rookie I've ever seen. I wish I was that good when I started."

It took only one swing around the league for Wilt to establish he had made it. He was acclaimed everywhere, to use Bill Russell's words, as "the best rookie ever."

Wilt's remarkable stamina, which enabled him to play a full 48 minutes of every game, was an important factor in his success. Most teams did not have a first string defender who could go the entire distance. Boston's Bill Russell was an exception.

In St. Louis, for instance, center Larry Foust, who was extremely effective in defending against big Wilt, did not have the physical strength to be a 48 minute man. Detroit's center, the towering Walter Dukes, sometimes dueled Chamberlain on a standoff basis, but he fouled often and was seldom around at game's end.

With the season one-quarter over, Wilt was averaging 36.5 points a game, a figure rival coaches had to marvel at. The all-time record was 29.2 points per game.

And Wilt was averaging 30 to 32 rebounds a game. The all-time season record was only 22.4.

Someone asked Ed Macauley, coach of the St. Louis Hawks, "How do you stop him, Ed?"

Macauley shrugged. "About all you can do is lock the door to the dressing room before he comes out," he answered.

10

Most Valuable

FOR PHILADELPHIA, 1959–1960 was the season of the Great Chase. From October, not long after the World Series, through the football season and the bowl games, through hockey season and all of the long winter, until March when baseballs were in the air again, the Warriors pursued the Celtics, but they never caught them.

Once or twice they came very close. In November for a time they were only a game and one-half behind but they fell back. Then in January, riding the crest of a 10 game winning streak, the Warriors barged to within two and one-half games of the Celts. Hurt by the loss of an injured Jim Loscutoff, Boston looked to be headed for a mild slump, but Cousy rallied the team and twice in one week they sent the Warriors reeling.

After that it became clear that Boston would finish first and Philadelphia second, and that was exactly what happened.

Philadelphia's lack of depth was a constant drawback to the team. When one of the starting five was injured, tired or simply the victim of an off night, there was no solid replacement available.

Over the year, Wilt performed with far greater success than anyone had dared anticipate.

One night in Madison Square Garden Wilt caged 58 points—the most ever scored by a player in the Garden. He dunked, tapped, hooked and rebounded like a dervish, even though double-teamed by Charlie Tyra and Richie Guerin through most of the second half. Later in the year he hit 58 again in a game against Detroit at Bethlehem, Pennsylvania.

Chamberlain did not merely set new league marks during the season, he devastated the record books and accounted for more "mosts" than most basketball players attain in a lifetime.

He scored 2,707 points over the year, topping by more than 600 Bob Pettit's league record set the year before. He averaged 37.6 points a game, also a new mark. He shattered the league's rebounding record, too, averaging 28 a game.

He became the first player in league history to score 50 points or more seven times in one season. He set new league marks in field goals, shots attempted, foul goals attempted, rebounds and tied for the most minutes played.

Not only did Wilt swish points through baskets at a clip never seen before, he also succeeded in getting the league's turnstiles to whirl at a happy pace. League attendance was up 24 percent over the previous year. Said a league official: "Wilt is responsible for 19 of that 24 percent."

Wilt was unanimously voted the league's No. 1 rookie *and* the Most Valuable Player by the New York Metropolitan Basketball Writers Association. He was the first player ever to receive both awards. "Very likely he will be the last," said one writer.

As the season's leading rookie, Wilt received the Hy Turkin Award, named after the late sportswriter of the New York *Daily News*. As the league's "MVP," he won the Sam Davis Award, named for the late cartoonist of the Long Island *Press*.

The U. S. Basketball Writers Association confirmed the opinion of the New York writers, and also named Wilt the league's Most Valuable Player. For this Chamberlain received the Podoloff Cup.

On the surface all looked perfect. Indeed it was not. Wilt was troubled—deeply troubled.

The main cause of his distress was that he felt professional basketball was not quite the game he had expected it to be. It had to do with the way he was being defensed. In professional ball, the rules made man-to-man defense obligatory. Yet it was Wilt's contention that the referees were allowing the defenses to sag on him, forming an illegal zone.

"They're not playing me man-on-man," he said. "They're playing me men-on-man.

"I asked one official why he didn't invoke the no-zone ruling. He told me, 'I haven't called a no-zone in this league in years. I'm not going to start now.' "

There is no doubt about it; the defenses did sag off on Wilt. Many methods were used to cut him down to normal size. He was boxed out. He was face-guarded. They ran on him. But mostly he was ganged up on. In fact, Boston, who could boast Bill Russell, was the only club that did not double-team or triple-team him.

Again Wilt used *Look* Magazine to billboard his complaints. The article was Part II of the arrangement he had made with the magazine during his final year at college.

"The National Basketball Association has two standards of officiating," Wilt charged in *Look*. "One for the league as a whole, another for me, Wilt Chamberlain."

Chamberlain's charges were scoffed at by most players and coaches, and from Maurice Podoloff, then President of the NBA, they brought a sharp rebuke. "I think the referees are doing the best job that can be done," Podoloff said. "I think Chamberlain better wait until he's been in the league a year or two before he can judge what's going on."

The tempest put a mental strain upon Wilt, but he was also suffering physically and it was the physical punishment that really distressed him.

It is not news that basketball as the professionals play it is a rough and rugged business. When you stretch for a rebound, there is body contact. It can't be helped; you hit and you get hit. Wilt fully realized this before he joined the Warriors. Each of the outstanding players of the day—Bob Pettit, Dolf Schayes and Bob Cousy—took his share of abuse. Wilt's complaint was that he was taking much more of a pounding than anyone else.

Neil Johnston, the Warriors' coach, urged Wilt to return the punishment in kind. "They're getting away with murder against Wilt," he said. "It would help if he would belt a few."

This is not to say that Wilt played the part of an innocent lamb completely. As Dolf Schayes once said, "He knew his way around elbows." But it was his coach's view that Wilt was never as aggressive as he should be.

Ike Gellis, sports editor of the New York *Post,* tried to give Wilt some advice about roughhousing. He told Wilt what had happened to Sweetwater Clifton of the New York Knickerbockers when he broke in. During an exhibition game against the Celtics, Sweets got involved with Bob Harris. Harris called him a dirty name and Sweets yelled at him, "Come out punching."

Harris threw the first punch. It missed. Sweets fired a fast one-two combination that didn't. "He knocked Harris dead in his tracks," said Gellis, and from that day on Sweets was one of the most respected men in the league.

Wilt listened, then shrugged. "But if I punch someone in the face, what does that prove?" he said. And he could not bring himself to retaliate with his fists.

The punishment that Wilt absorbed was not trivial. After games his ribs often showed bruises from well planted elbows.

Elbows were to be expected, but some other offenses weren't. Early in the season his left foot was painfully injured in a game against the Hawks in St. Louis. The foot swelled up and Wilt had to miss a game.

Later in the year, again in St. Louis, Chamberlain caught Clyde Lovellette's elbow in the mouth. It struck with such force it drove some teeth up into his gums. Terrible pain and swelling were the result and Wilt couldn't eat solid food for days.

He continued to play—wearing a grotesque face mask for protection. Then the injury was aggravated in a game against New York when Wilt was struck on the mouth by Willie Naulls' elbow. After that, two teeth had to be extracted.

Naturally, Wilt was disappointed by the fact that the Warriors had not won the Eastern Division championship. But the Division playoffs lay ahead, and the Warriors looked upon these as an opportunity to dethrone the Celts. Wilt felt this way, of course. But he also looked upon the upcoming games as still another test in his pride-filled and often grueling campaign to prove himself.

11

Playoffs

IT MUST BE THAT, for the players at least, the playoffs to determine the team champion in the National Basketball Association each year are a rather unreasonable extension of a long season.

The basketball year begins with the exhibition games and most teams arrange about 18 of these. Then comes the regular 80 game slate, a coast-to-coast schedule, worked out on a crazy quilt pattern that has teams jumping hither and yon and sometimes playing as many as six games in six nights in half a dozen different cities.

It is not all packed arenas and wildly cheering crowds. Far from it. It is much more a succession of dreary hotel rooms, cheerless restaurants and the gray-green dinginess of league dressing rooms.

It is trying to sleep in too-small airplane seats or on a bench in an airport waiting room. It is being away from home—maybe even on Christmas Day. Late in the season, it often means playing with a painful injury. It is being tired—always tired.

By the time the 80 game schedule ends, the players are dog-weary. Then come the playoffs, and for some teams this can mean as many as 19 additional games.

The playoffs involve the top three teams in each division of the league and any one of these three, by winning, can become the division and then the league champion. In a certain sense, this arrangement makes the 80 game schedule somewhat meaningless, rather no more than a warm-up for the playoffs. "We play all year to eliminate the Knicks," is the way Wilt has expressed it.

Players' salary paychecks stop when the playoffs begin. Instead, they draw from a playoff pool. For 1959–1960, this fund was $100,000. (Two years later it was increased to $125,000.)

Of this sum, $2,000 is paid to the team that finishes in first place in the division, and this team also draws a bye while the second and third place teams compete in the semi-finals. So there is a mighty striving to finish first, not so much for the team prize of $2,000; instead, that solid week of glorious rest is the goal.

Of the $100,000, in 1960, each team in the semi-finals was to receive $4,000. Then, by defeating Boston, the semi-finalists could earn another $9,000. Should they go all the way and become league champions, they could divide an additional $17,000. Indeed, the incentive was there.

For Philadelphia, the playoffs shaped up this way: they had to defeat third place Syracuse (in a two-out-of-three series) for the right to meet Boston (in a four-out-of-seven series.) If successful against Boston, they would then take on the Western Division winner for the league title.

The first goal was to dispose of Syracuse. The Nationals had talent enough to keep the Warriors hopping. Up front they had Dolf Schayes, George Yardly and Johnny Kerr, a trio often judged as the league's most potent marksmen. Larry Costello, Hal Greer and Al Bianchi were featured in the backcourt, and they gave the Nats great speed and playmaking skill.

It was essential that the Warriors win the first game of the series being played on their home court, Convention Hall, for they figured on losing the second contest which was scheduled for Syracuse. The Nationals were just about invincible at home.

The Warriors did win the first game. Paul Arizin sparked the team with 40 points. Wilt netted 35 points, rebounded well and was effective in keeping Dolf Schayes in check. Then the teams went to Syracuse where the Nationals won as expected and the series was even. The game at Syracuse was a rugged one for Wilt. He and Johnny Kerr battered bitterly for the full 48 minutes, and Kerr held Wilt to a lowly 7 points.

Back in Philadelphia the next night for the crucial final game, Wilt rose to the occasion. He exploded with 53 points, an all-time playoff record. His fall-away speciality and his spinning jumps enabled him to get 16 points in the first 10 minutes, and late in the second quarter he struck with eight straight points to put the Warriors 19 ahead. By the fourth quarter, the issue was no longer in doubt. The only matter to be decided was when would Wilt get his record. It came on a two-handed jump with about five minutes to play.

"Was this the best game you ever played?" Wilt was asked after the game. "I don't know if I've ever shot better or not," he said, "but I know I never played so well under such pressure and when it meant so much."

Now the division finals were ahead. In Boston, resting like fat cats, the Celtics waited.

Unfortunately for the Warriors, the series opened at the Boston Garden where the Celtics were virtually unconquerable. Amazingly, only twice during the entire year had they lost before their hometown fans.

The Warriors were not up to reversing the tide. They were beaten, 111–105, though Wilt out-maneuvered Bill Russell to score 42 points. The difference between the two teams was most glaring in the backcourt. In this department the Celtics, sparked by Cousy, outscored the Warriors, 54–31.

The turning point of the playoff series came with the next game. It was played at Convention Hall and a record crowd of 12,581 was on hand for the frenzied proceedings.

Midway in the second quarter, Wilt and Boston's bruising Tommy Heinsohn jostled one another under the boards. Out of the elbowing erupted a war. For the first time in his career, Wilt started punching. His arms flailed like a giant windmill. The crowd screamed and players from both teams flooded out on to the floor.

As they struggled to halt the battle, Wilt let go with a roundhouse right. It missed Heinsohn's chin by inches (if it had struck him it would have flattened him for sure), but connected with someone else's hand or elbow. Wilt winced in pain and grabbed his knuckles. No one realized it at the time, but serious damage had been done.

The NBA usually takes an extremely tolerant view of such antics and this time was no exception. Referee Mendy Rudolph charged each player with an offensive foul. Neither player was ejected. Neither was fined.

Play resumed. Both teams were very obviously weary and below par all evening. Ball handling was careless. Passes went awry. At length the Warriors outfumbled the Celtics, 115–110. Paul Arizin's 30 points was the Philadelphia high. Wilt gathered 29 points, but only 9 of these after his fray with Hein-sohn.

Following the game, the knuckles of Wilt's hand were puffed and painful. He played the next day in Boston—but just barely.

His hand was still swollen and whenever he moved it, the knuckles were struck with a stabbing pain. Never once during the game did he come close to attaining his usual form and when Neil Johnston went in to replace him in the third quarter, Chamberlain had caged a pitiful 12 points. The hapless Warriors were never in contention and the Celts trounced them, 120–90.

After the game Wilt was taken to Massachusetts General Hospital to have his hand X-rayed. The X rays showed no broken bones. "There are several con-tusions and bruises of the phalangeal metacarpal joints on the second and third fingers of the right hand," said the report. In non-technical terms this meant Wilt's knuckles had been injured and were painfully swollen. Wilt didn't need X rays to tell him that.

There was a day of rest and then the teams met for the fourth game, once again in Philadelphia. Wilt showed signs of returning to his "most valuable" form but he was still below par and the Celtics won without too much difficulty. Now, with their 3–1 advantage, they had a strangle hold on the championship.

For the fifth game, played at the Boston Garden, Wilt was in peak form. He scored 50 points, a record for the Garden, on 22 field goals and six foul shots, and the Warriors won it, 128–107.

Philadelphia's hopes flared. "Any time you beat Boston at home by 20 points, you've got a chance," said Neil Johnston. But in Philadelphia just 48 hours later, the Celtics delivered the crusher.

It was a heartbreaking defeat for the Warriors.

They fought every inch of the way and Wilt hooked up in a fierce tooth-and-nail struggle with Bill Russell.

Neither team could build much of an advantage and the game came down to the last 11 seconds with the score tied at 117-all. Philadelphia's Guy Rodgers, the hottest man on the court with 31 points, was fouled and awarded two free throws. He missed them both. The huge crowd gasped.

Now it was Boston's ball and the Celts quickly called a time out to set their strategy. Bill Sharman threw the ball in for the Celtics. Cousy grabbed it and rifled a pass down court to Tommy Heinsohn. Heinsohn fired back to Sharman whose jump shot goal had tied the score. Now Sharman jumped again. This time he missed and the Warriors swarmed for the rebound.

As the ball sprang from the board, Tommy Heinsohn leaped high and clubbed it back toward the basket. The ball went in. And what was worse, it swished through the cords to the accompaniment of the final buzzer. To the Warriors, the klaxon's moan was like a death knell.

With sickening suddenness the game—the season, in fact—was over. A desperate play in the final second had decided the outcome of the long, long struggle.

The huge crowd sat in stunned silence. Out on the court, the Celtic players mobbed Sharman (for at first they thought he had scored the final goal) and then Heinsohn.

The Warriors were bewildered. They milled about as if they were lost.

In the Philadelphia dressing room Wilt sat dejectedly on a bench in front of his locker. The quick defeat had a bitter sting. He was more worn and weary than he had every been before in his whole life. It was then he made the announcement that was to shock the whole world of sports.

12

"I Quit"

"I'LL NEVER PLAY BASKETBALL in the NBA again. This is my last game. This is it."

With these words Wilt quit.

Rumors had been circulating for weeks that Wilt would retire at the end of the season. The players in the league and the sportswriters who covered the teams fully realized that Wilt was tired of being roughed up. The feeling was, however, that when the season was over and Wilt's bruises had healed, he would shelve his retirement plans.

Wilt's announcement astounded basketball observers. In all of sports, there had been nothing before to compare with it. Players had retired before, of course. But never at the age of 23.

The story that Wilt was going to call it quits first appeared in the New York *Post*.

"Right after the playoff game I went into the Philadelphia dressing room and spoke to Wilt," recalls Ike Gellis, sports editor of the paper. "I said to him,

'Is it true, Wilt? Are you going to quit?' He said it was."

"I hate to go out like this," Chamberlain told Gellis. "I was hoping we could go all the way and I could have quit a winner."

What were Wilt's plans for the future? They were extremely indefinite. "I'm going to free-lance," he said.

Wilt could announce nothing clear-cut and rumors abounded. It was reported he was going to take a public relations post with a West Coast brewery, or promote a touring track and field exhibition or play basketball again with the Globetrotters.

Abe Saperstein was planning to launch a new basketball league and there were reports that Wilt would join the Los Angeles entry in the new circuit.

At any rate, the announcement triggered a mighty furore.

"It's a shock to me," said Eddie Gottlieb. "He did talk to me about quitting when we started a contract discussion earlier in the week, but I was sure he had changed his mind by the time we had finished."

Maurice Podoloff, then President of the league, was shocked, too. "I never thought it would happen," he said. "The unfortunate aspect of the whole matter is that the boy hasn't even come into his prime. I'm sure that he would have broken all the records next season that he created during the past one."

Around the league, the reaction to Wilt's retirement plans could be characterized as mixed. Many of the players were overjoyed at the thought of not having to face Wilt on the basketball court again, but their enthusiasm was dimmed when they realized it was Chamberlain who had been largely responsible for the tremendous increase in the league's attendance. And professional athletes know that when gate receipts rise, salaries are likely to follow.

A few days after the final playoff game, Wilt appeared at the annual awards banquet of the Philadelphia sportswriters. Before the evening's program began, he repeated to a group of writers that he would never play in the NBA again.

He also denied that he had introduced a racial issue into his decision to quit. Indeed, in announcing his plans to Ike Gellis, Wilt had not even hinted that anything remotely resembling racial prejudice had anything to do with his decision.

What he did say was that if he continued playing and was unable to keep his equilibrium, "It might be bad for me and my race." That was the way the original story had it.

But in the stories that followed, the sense of what Wilt had said was twisted and the emphasis was shifted so as to make the matter of race relations appear as a salient factor in Wilt's decision.

The erroneous story was carried far and wide. Bob Cousy read it in a Massachusetts newspaper. Speaking in his capacity as the NBA players' representative, he issued a sharply-worded statement in answer to charges Wilt had never made.

"Racial issues have never had anything to do with my quitting college or the NBA," was what Wilt told the Philadelphia sportswriters in an effort to clear away the confusion.

In the weeks that followed, Wilt's family and his friends urged him to reconsider his decision. Letters came in from every part of the country asking him to change his mind. During the summer he toured again with the Globetrotters, and he was surprised by the number of people in Europe who wanted him to continue his professional career.

Wilt's decision to quit was not a well-reasoned one. At the time—in those moments of terrible disappointment after the playoff defeat—and with the woes of the season weighing heavily upon him, the decision did not make bad sense. It was the sure way to prevent any such ills in the future.

But in the weeks and months that followed, Wilt saw clearly how rashly he had acted. He knew he could not quit.

With the contract that Gottlieb had offered him, it would have been terribly unprofitable for him to retire. Also, the question was being asked now whether he was simply a one-year sensation or a star of solid talents. He wanted to return to re-establish his eminence. By mid-summer he was ready to come back.

13

Foul Line Fiasco

FROM THE FOUL LINE most tall players prefer the two-hand overhand free throw. Since it is one of their specialty shots from the field, using it when shooting fouls helps in achieving an overall proficiency with the weapon.

It's not difficult to master the shot from the foul line, say the instruction books. All you have to do is hold the ball loosely in your finger tips, square your shoulders and hips to the basket, get solidly balanced and then fire.

The great value of the free throw is recognized by every coach and player. In high school, long hours are spent practicing the art, and some coaches recommend that fledgling players should make at least 50 free throws every day during their practice drills.

To Wilt Chamberlain, success from the free throw line has been terribly elusive. A good high school player averages about .666 from the foul line, and more nights than not Wilt would gladly settle for that degree of competence.

During his first season as a professional, Wilt was awarded more free throws than any other player in the league, an amazing 991 of them, an average of 14 every game. Of these he hit only 577, a minuscule 58 percent.

By high school standards, Wilt's average was merely below par, but by the professional norm—.734 was the 1959–1960 average from the foul line—Wilt's performance was appalling. Incredibly, Wilt showed a better shooting percentage on field goals than on fouls.

In Wilt's defense, it should be pointed out that he played part of his rookie year with a knee injured while performing in Europe with the Globetrotters the summer before the season opened. The injury prevented him from using a natural motion on foul line tosses and this is one reason his accuracy may have been poor.

Wilt's aptitude from the free throw line, a serious problem during the 1959–1960 season, reached calamitous proportions the next year.

The Warrior team of 1960–1961 was somewhat changed from the previous season. Guy Rodgers and Tom Gola returned as Philadelphia's slick backcourt combination, and an addition at guard was Al Attles, a fast and promising rookie. Paul Arizin's hawk-eye talents up front were expected to be supplemented by those of Ed Conlin, who had been obtained from St. Louis in a trade that sent Woody Sauldsberry to the Hawks. Swift, mobile and versatile, Conlin was expected to hold in the backcourt as well as the forecourt.

While the Warriors looked a bit better, so—unfortunately—did the Celtics. Jim Loscutoff, out for part of the previous season, was back and in good health. Boston's first draft choice, Tom Sanders, showed well in exhibition games, so well it appeared he would be receiving starting assignments. Cousy, Russell, Sharman, Heinsohn and the Jones boys, Sam and K. C., were all returning.

After they had defeated the Warriors in the divisional playoff, the Celtics had gone on to beat the Hawks quite handily in the finals. Few observers entertained any doubts that the Celtics were the best in the business during 1959–1960. In the year just ahead, they rated as improved over that.

For the Warriors, the season got off to a brilliant start. They downed the Nationals in the opener at hostile War Memorial Stadium in Syracuse. Next they flattened the Celtics—and in Boston.

After that the team really began to soar, with the new players, Conlin and Attles, important factors in the Warriors' spurt. In a brief home stand, the team drubbed Los Angeles, then Cincinnati and then Detroit. Against the Pistons, Wilt sparked the attack with 44 points and a remarkable 39 rebounds.

Wilt was playing a brand of ball that was noticeably better. While he wasn't scoring quite as much as he had the year before, at least in the early stages of the season, he was passing off more and was chasing his man more on defense. He showed more skill in eluding defenders when trying to get back from in between to his rebound position under the defensive board. He had also come up with a right-hand hook shot.

He was more confident than he had been the year before, and he himself felt he was playing better even though his scoring average was down a bit. "I know I'm giving more this year," he said.

With their proud five game winning streak in hand, the Warriors headed for Boston. There, in the first game of a doubleheader, they handed Detroit a second thrashing. They whipped Los Angeles a second time in a game played in St. Louis and, before returning home, they stopped at Madison Square Garden where they trounced the Knicks. In Philadelphia against the

Hawks, Wilt caught fire in the second half of a close game, and struck with a sensational 10 field goals in 10 attempts that carried the Warriors to their ninth straight win.

The very next night the Warriors met the Hawks again, but this time in St. Louis. There the Hawks brought the Warriors to earth. Philadelphia was travel weary from almost a week of hop, skip and jump scheduling and their playing showed it. Passes were mishandled time and time again, but the team's most glaring deficiency was at the foul line. The club missed 20 out of 37 free throw shots. Wilt hit only 6 of 12, and this was a game the Warriors had lost by only two points.

During their nine game winning streak, Philadelphia's play was often characterized by dreadful showings from the free throw line. Almost always Wilt was the worst offender. In a game against Detroit, he missed 10 of 10. But this particular performance, and some others almost as disappointing, were hardly noticed because the Warriors were winning. However, once the team began to lose, the inadequacy shone forth like a bright sun.

The Warriors lost in Cincinnati to the Royals. Wilt was 4 for 11 from the foul line. The Pistons beat them easily in Detroit. Wilt got 5 of 13.

When the Warriors returned to Convention Hall, Syracuse handed them their fourth loss in a row, 106–105. Wilt was an awful 9 for 27 from the line.

"It's ridiculous," said Syracuse's Dolf Schayes after the game. "Any high school kid could do better than that."

The Warriors had a losing streak going that now reached four games, and during that period Wilt had been able to make only 24 shots in 63 foul line attempts, a depressing .379 average. His morale was even lower.

"I keep saying, 'Don't let it bother you; don't let it

bother you.' But whenever you find yourself saying that, you know it *is* bothering you."

Warrior coach Neil Johnston felt that Wilt's style of shooting from the outside hampered him in his attempts from the free throw line. "He has a natural tendency to put English on the ball when he shoots his one-handers," Johnston pointed out. "When he tries fouls this hurts him."

Wilt experimented with a number of different styles in an effort to pull out of his slump (a plan that probably did him more harm than good). He tried positioning himself just to the left of the foul line, shooting at an angle toward the hoop. He thought the way in which he was holding his thumb might be putting too much English on the ball, so he tried changing its position. Nothing seemed to work.

Every coach and every player in the league had an opinion on Wilt's problem. Fans by the hundreds wrote letters offering counsel.

Midway in the season Eddie Gottlieb was so distressed over the problem he arranged to hire a tutor for Wilt. His name was Cy Kaselman, and he could boast a peerless record as a foul shooter. A veteran of the Philadelphia Spahs of the American Basketball League of the 1920's, Kaselman, then 51, hit an incredible 247 out of 261 free throws one season. He could even make them blindfolded.

At first Wilt rejected the idea of a private instructor. The thought embarrassed him.

But Kaselman told Wilt that he was being fouled intentionally because of his inability to score from the free throw line. "If these fellows thought you were going to make your shot, you'd get hit a lot less," he told Wilt.

Kaselman also appealed to Wilt's pride. "People are laughing at you," he told him. That argument clinched it; Wilt would take the lessons.

Kaselman had detected a hitch in Wilt's motion that seemed to be the heart of the problem. At the bottom of his downward swing, there was a momentary pause. This destroyed the rhythm of his delivery and, as Kaselman put it, "Foul shooting is based on rhythm."

Wilt's instructor got him to go back to an underhand motion and he worked to build the big man's confidence. It needed building.

"What do you think of when you step up to the line?" Kaselman asked. Wilt answered he thought about missing.

Slowly Wilt's free performance began to improve. Toward the end of the season, it edged over 50 percent.

It didn't get too much higher. It never has. Foul shooting to this day continues to be perhaps Wilt's most glaring weakness.

He tries to make light of the failing. "At least I'm consistent," he says. "And consistency is the mark of a pro."

However, the inadequacy causes him deep concern, and when he steps to the line his face reflects the agony he feels. It does not improve matters that fans around the league hoot and holler when Wilt gets ready to shoot; when he makes a shot, they yell derisively.

Wilt gets some consolation from the fact that Bill Russell, his arch competitor, is as poor a foul shooter as he is.

Another consoling fact, and a much more important one, is Wilt's ability to deliver under pressure. When the game is in its late stages and every point looms crucial, Wilt's concentration becomes fierce and he often nets free throws with Kaselman-like consistency. That *is* the mark of a pro.

14

"They're All the Same on Payday"

FOUL SHOOTING was not the least of the problems during Wilt's sophomore year as a professional. There came to be a lack of harmony between Wilt and the Warrior coach, Neil Johnston; as the season progressed, this problem took on monumental proportions.

One night Wilt came into the dressing room at half-time and Johnston told him, "Wilt, you've got to start playing Lovelette closer."

Wilt snapped back his answer. "I'm trying to rebound and cover my man, too. You never tell Arizin or Gola or anybody else they have to play their man closer," he said.

"Wilt," Johnston replied coolly, "they're not making $65,000 a year like you are."

Wilt felt the reference to his salary was uncalled for. He exploded. "We said some rough things to one another," he recalls.

That was only one instance. There were other disputes and in a number of them Wilt's fierce pride was injured. Sometimes days would pass with Wilt and his coach barely speaking to one another.

For his part, Johnston protested that Wilt enjoyed certain privileges not given the other players. He reported to friends that Wilt was shown favoritism by the front office. It was Johnston's theory that, "Every player should be treated exactly the same—except on payday."

Naturally, the breakdown in communication between Wilt and Johnston influenced other members of the Warriors. Team morale had to suffer and it did.

It must be said that the players of any professional basketball team—the players of any team in any sport, for that matter—often display feelings of displeasure and discontent. Some grumbling is normal. The team is, after all, simply 10 individuals. Each has his own problem or problems.

If you were to call a meeting of any given basketball team, professional or otherwise, and pose the question, "How can this team be improved?", it's likely the answers you would get would in part, at least, reflect the same age-old gripes. It would be normal for the forwards to complain they were not getting fed enough. Backcourt men would protest they were not being permitted enough shots. Players that warmed the bench would complain about not playing.

When a team has a Wilt Chamberlain as its leading member, a player whose talents far surpass everyone else's, and whose salary does likewise, the feelings of dissatisfaction are very likely to be greater than normal. Players are human; they are susceptible to envy. So the coach of such a team must not only have the ability to team basketball's techniques and tactics, he must also have an inordinate amount of skill in dealing with people.

And Wilt himself is a special problem. Indeed, he is

a sensitive person. If you stood 7 feet plus in a 5 feet 10 inch world, if you had been called "freak" in at least a dozen languages, you would be sensitive. You would be thin-skinned; often you would be silent and even sulky.

For the Warriors the four game losing streak that followed the long string of victories was the season's turning point. After it they were never able to gain their peak form again.

Often the team lacked spirit in offensive rebounding. They seldom practiced screens or picks. Sometimes they looked totally disorganized.

In some games Wilt shot whenever he got the ball. Or sometimes he would be open for a feed under the basket, but the ball wouldn't be passed to him. He would plead for the ball, and when he was passed up and the shot popped, a look of disgust would cloud his face.

After the mid-season break for the league All Star Game (a game in which Wilt was held to only two field goals), the Celtics began to pull away from the Warriors and every other team in the league. The season, which had begun in such glorious fashion, was tailing off in ignominious style.

Even Eddie Gottlieb could not right the team. Sometimes their play infuriated him. "I'd tell them they weren't playing like a team. I'd tell them they were playing like 10 guys I picked up off the street." Sometimes the upbraiding would be effective and the club would perk up for a game or two, but more often it had no effect at all.

Through the latter stages of the season Wilt was often unhappy and he showed it. Words like "distant," "gloomy" and "moody" were being used to describe him.

Despite the fact that Wilt was often dispirited, his

personal scoring achievements soared to new heights. His most gaudy feat came late in the season at Philadelphia's Palestra where he hit a whopping 67 points in a game against the hapless Knicks. A career high for Wilt, the total was just four shy of the NBA record of 71 then held by Elgin Baylor. Chamberlain scored with dips and dunks, with jumpers and fadeaways. He hit from the front and from the side. "Wilt set the cords aflame," said one observer. His shooting average was a sizzling 75.7. From the foul line he was 13 for 17.

Shortly before the end of the season, Wilt reached another career milestone when he became the first player in professional history to hit 3,000 points for a season. He broke the 3,000 barrier in a game against the Detroit Pistons in Allen County Memorial Stadium in Fort Wayne, Indiana. The date was March 10.

In the second quarter he banked a right-handed hook from about 15 feet out. A tremendous roar came up from the crowd of 10,018 when the ball swished through the net. Then the game was halted, the public address system confirmed what everybody knew and Detroit coach Dick McGuire presented Wilt with the ball. It was the only bright spot of the night as the Warriors took another drubbing.

Wilt also won renown during the season as the Warriors' "iron man." When he was called to the side lines by Johnston during the season's last game, his removal ended a playing streak of 45 consecutive games without relief. "Workhorse Wilt" was what some observers had dubbed him.

Wilt broke 10 all-time records over the season. He wound up with 3,033 points, an average of 38. 3 points for the 79 games in which he played.

In addition to scoring and averaging, he took down the season records for most field goal attempts, most field goals scored, highest field goal percentage, most rebounds, most free throws attempted and most games scoring 50 points or more.

Yet when the season ended the Warriors were a distant second to the Celtics.

Again in the preliminary playoff round, the Warriors were matched against the Syracuse Nationals, with the winner to face the Celtics for the division championship.

The team was able to muster a fair amount of enthusiasm for the playoffs, yet in the first game, played on their home court, they looked completely disorganized, like Gottlieb's "10 guys picked off the street." They never led and the Nationals won easily.

The second game, played at Syracuse, was more of a thriller, but the outcome was the same. The third game was a replay of the first.

Wilt made his way slowly to the dressing room after the final contest. He could take consolation only in the fact that the dreary season was over.

The day after the playoffs ended, Neil Johnston predicted some changes were going to be made.

His prediction held true. A few days later, *he* resigned.

15

Businessman

WHILE WILT CHAMBERLAIN'S talents as a *complete* basketball player have been questioned by his team-mates, opposing players, coaches, fans and segments of the press, his aptitude in matters financial has never been disputed by anyone.

This story serves as an example.

Following a playoff game in Syracuse on a cold March night in 1962, the Warriors voted to take a bus back to Philadelphia rather than wait for a plane flight the next day.

As they settled into their seats, one of the players suggested they form a sweepstakes on the number of miles the bus would travel from the War Memorial Auditorium in Syracuse to the airport in Philadelphia where most of their cars were parked. Each of the players began picking a figure and putting a dollar in the pool. The closest guess would win it all.

When it came to Wilt's turn there was $8 in the

fund. He did some figuring with a pencil and paper and then announced he was putting $44 in the pot, and he called off the numbers he was taking including every mile between 283 and 336, except those which had already been taken.

At intervals during the long trip he watched the mileage indicator, and by the time the bus reached Wilmington, it was obvious to everyone that Wilt could not lose (though Eddie Gottlieb threatened to order the driver to meander through the streets of Philadelphia until *his* number came up).

When Wilt pocketed his $8 profit some of the players couldn't understand how he could risk $44 to win $8. To Wilt the reasoning was plain. He looked upon his venture as an investment, one that paid close to an 18 percent return. As a businessman, Wilt knew that any time you can get an 18 percent return on your money, you are doing very well indeed. And Wilt is, first and foremost, a businessman.

Wilt has always shied away from discussions of his income as a basketball player and of his financial situation in general. But one thing is certain; he has come a long, long way since the days he delivered orders for Bert's grocery or bussed tables at Kutshers.

The late Ike Richman, general counsel of the Philadelphia 76ers, and the man who served as Wilt's attorney until his death in 1966, once said, "Wilt is better off financially than any other professional athlete. When he retires from competitive sports, he could be a millionaire."

Wilt will neither confirm or deny such statements. "I've made some good investments; I've made some bad ones," is about all he will say.

It should be mentioned that Wilt has always had a profound appreciation for money. It was an overriding factor in his decision to quit college and join the Globetrotters. It was the prime consideration in his coming out of "retirement" after his rookie year. In both cases, the money proffered was just too much to turn down.

Wilt likes money for what it can do. He likes to be able to travel abroad. He likes to be able to wear stylish and expensive custom clothes. Money enables him to drive a $23,000 purple Bentley, to have a four and one-half room luxury Manhattan apartment and to visit the town's chic nightspots.

This is not to imply that Chamberlain is wasteful or extravagant with money. Indeed he is not. While he permits himself many of those things that give him personal comfort and satisfaction, the great bulk of his earnings are invested with an astuteness that befits someone well beyond his age and experience.

It is all part of the picture. Business investment he accepts as a personal challenge just like putting the shot or arm wrestling Bill Nieder. It is a world where height offers not the slightest advantage and therefore one wherein Wilt wants to show he can be pre-eminent.

Will Wilt, as Ike Richman predicted, be a millionaire when he retires? It could happen—and easily.

The financial "empire" that Wilt is building for himself is founded on his salary. This has never been small.

When he signed with the Philadelphia Warriors in 1959, his contract assured him an income that would make him the highest paid performer in the National Basketball Association. Before Wilt joined the league, Bob Cousy was said to be the highest paid star, with earnings reported at $25,000 a year. Wilt's contract, according to Ed Gottlieb, "was in excess of $30,000," which was more money than Gottlieb had paid for the entire franchise not many years before. Some sources claimed that Wilt received as much as $55,000 during his rookie year.

So Wilt's earnings started high. After his rookie year they skyrocketed.

In the summer of 1960, following a six-week tour

with the Harlem Globetrotters, and after he had changed his mind about quitting, Wilt signed a three-year contract with the Warriors. According to Gottlieb, the document made Wilt "the highest paid athlete in sports."

At that time Willie Mays of the San Francisco Giants held down that munificent role. He was being paid an estimated $85,000 a year.

Wilt's contract with Philadelphia guaranteed him a base salary and contained bonus arrangements that added considerably to the total sum. All involved admitted it was a complicated document, one that well befitted the talents of the several Philadelphia lawyers that put it together.

It is safe to say that during the years the contract was in effect, Chamberlain's income hovered around the $100,000 mark each year. In the years that followed, his income was never less than that figure, and often quite a bit above it.

What happens to Wilt's salary each year? Of course, the Internal Revenue Service skims off a great part. Most of what remains is invested.

Beginning in 1959, the year Wilt signed with the Globetrotters, he has plunked down annually from $12,000 to $15,000 in mutual funds.

When you purchase shares in a mutual investment fund, what you are doing is allowing experts to buy stocks and bonds of their selection for you. For their expertise, they are paid a fee.

"It's the lazy man's way to save," is the way Wilt has characterized it. He never sees the money. It comes right out of his salary.

When Wilt's basketball days are over, the various funds in which he has invested are expected to yield him a fancy retirement income.

The most imposing of all of Wilt's many and varied investments is a 40-unit apartment house in Los Angeles. It is valued at $600,000 and is called the Villa Chamberlain. The story of how it came to be reveals that Chamberlain has as much talent in the business world as he displays under the boards.

Wilt purchased the land upon which the apartment stands, one of the last large plots in West Los Angeles, in 1960 for a reported $65,000. "I wasn't quite sure what I was going to do with it," Wilt said, "but I always felt that real estate in California could be a good investment." At length Wilt decided to have an apartment building constructed on the site and in 1962 he started to build.

Villa Chamberlain is just short of being luxurious. The one and two bedroom apartments rent for $110 to $150 a month. The development includes patios, a recreation room and a heated swimming pool.

The apartment is managed by Wilt's mother and father who moved from Philadelphia to superintend the investment. Chamberlain admits to having a quarter of a million dollars in the land and building.

Wilt also owns an apartment building in New York City. This he purchased in 1962. Located at 142nd Street and Riverside Drive, the seven-story 32-unit structure is valued at $240,000. He also owns two houses in Philadelphia that he rents out.

One of Wilt's investments is somewhat on the exotic side. It is a nightclub in New York City's Harlem named Small's Paradise. Wilt, in partnership with James McDougal, purchased the club in 1959.

Small's was a fabled landmark of the Roaring Twenties but the club's brilliance had long faded by the time Wilt arrived upon the scene. He immediately refurbished it inside and out to convert it into a rendezvous for athletes and show business people. He renamed it "Big Wilt's Small's Paradise" and a gaudy neon sign, its letters almost as tall as Wilt himself, proclaim the name. After the 1959–1960 basketball season, Wilt spent as much as 18 hours a day there learning the trade.

Small's has become a roaring success under Chamberlain. One source says income has tripled since he became owner. On weekends cars triple park outside on Seventh Avenue, and crowds jam in like the place was Boston Garden at playoff time.

Jokingly, Wilt has on occasions threatened to throw over his basketball career to become "an assistant bottle opener" at Small's.

Wilt also used to be part owner in a Los Angeles night club named Basin Street West. It was a much more modest investment than that represented by the sprawling Small's layout, but it did not pan out.

Chamberlain has also allowed himself investments that must be classed as frivolous. Racehorses, for instance.

In 1959 Wilt purchased what he has described as "an old broken-down horse." His name was Spooky Cadet and he cost Wilt $3,500.

The first time Spooky Cadet raced under Wilt's colors, all of Wilt's friends bet on him. The horse finished third and most of the people who bet lost money. Not Wilt. He got a part of the winner's purse because the horse finished third.

Racehorses provided Wilt with his first losing venture in business. In 1961 he purchased two broodmares, but neither of them would foal. He paid $5,000 each for them, but he was able to sell them for $7,000 each a year and a half later. However, the profit from the sale covered only a portion of the two horses' board and feed bills.

Wilt has had much better fortune with trotters and pacers. He owns shares of several. In 1963 he had Pace-A-Breeze, then the four-year-old American Trotting Champion. During 1965 he owned 20 percent of

Rivaltime, rated that year as the second best three-year-old pacer in the country.

Wilt is also a partner in the National All Sports Camp at Kutshers' Camp Anawana in Monticello, New York. Training in basketball is the stock in trade here; the fee is $125 per week per youngster.

In more recent years, Wilt has been able to accrue much more than just hot dog money from personal appearances, endorsements and the like. Wilt turns down many speaking engagements, each with a fancy fee attached, because they infringe on his private time to which he attaches a high value.

His salary; his stocks, bonds and mutual funds; his apartment buildings and rental houses; the nightclubs; the harness horses; and the basketball youth camp—it is estimated that they bring Wilt more than $200,000 a year.

His friends and relatives recall that Wilt, even as a youngster, was energetic and industrious. Before he was 10 years old he went to work for a neighborhood iceman, helping deliver the frozen blocks throughout the Haddington community. Later he worked for a milkman, and helped sell newspapers. His sister Barbara (now Mrs. Barbara Lewis of Los Angeles) recalls he was able to get such jobs because he was strong and very tall for his age.

Wilt probably inherited his business acumen from his father. During Wilt's childhood, Mr. Chamberlain was employed as a janitor by the Curtis Publishing Company. Though his income was slight, he made it stretch. Indeed, raising nine youngsters on a janitor's income requires the most astute type of money management.

Wilt is as generous with his money as he is wise. He will put a $100 bill on the bar and watch his friends drink it up while he sips a soft drink. About New York

City, where he now lives, doormen, waiters and cab drivers speak of him as a heavy tipper.

Yet neither Wilt's large and regular paychecks, nor the income or the equity he has built in his investments have given him any real sense of financial security. In his right trousers pocket, he invariably carries a thick wad of bills, of which the outer few are hundreds.

Ike Richman used to explain the habit dated to Wilt's boyhood days and the financial rigors he suffered. "If there was a time you never had any, you can never have too much," Richman said.

Richman used to warn Wilt: "Someday somebody's going to hit you over the head and rob you for that roll." To which Wilt replied, "If anybody's going to hit me over the head, he'll have to get a ladder first. And when I see somebody coming after me with a ladder, I'll know what's on his mind."

The fact that Wilt is well on his way to becoming the world's first 7 foot millionaire has naturally worked wonders for his self-confidence. For the type of money Wilt deals in, his psyche can absorb a lot of pop-eyed stares.

It is as Jim Murray of the Los Angeles *Times* put it: "When someone asks, 'How's the weather up there, Wilt?' Wilt can smile and say, 'Just fine. Smells just like money.'"

16

For the Record

WHEN HE AGREED to join the Warriors late in the summer of 1960, no college coach in all the country was held in greater esteem than Francis Joseph McGuire of the University of North Carolina. Over the nine years of McGuire's tenure, the Tar Heels had been consistently a national basketball power. He had developed half-a-dozen All American players and, in the 1956–1957 season, his team had turned in a perfect 32 game season and won the NCAA championship, with Wilt and his University of Kansas teammates the victims.

Born in New York City, the son of an Irish cop, the genial yet two-fisted McGuire built his strong teams by recruiting the best basketball players from the areas in and around New York City, and then molding them into a winning organization by feeding them large doses of organization and discipline. On the basis of the Warriors' showing over the previous season, these were qualities the team required in a most desperate way.

Owners of professional basketball teams, particularly the Knicks, in addition to the Warriors, began pursuing McGuire shortly after officials of the University of North Carolina announced a de-emphasis of basketball in the wake of a bribe scandal that implicated two Tar Heel players. After a struggle, the Warriors won out.

At a press conference announcing the signing of the new coach, Ed Gottlieb said, "We kept after him for two and one-half months. He turned down two offers before signing." Gottlieb also stated that McGuire had signed a contract that would make him, "one of the highest paid coaches in college or professional basketball."

The job that McGuire had ahead of him was plain for everyone to see. In specific terms, what he had to do was translate the great skills of Wilt Chamberlain into victories for the team.

"Wilt," said McGuire when the two met at the Warriors' training camp at Hershey, Pennsylvania, "I have two goals this season. I hope we win the championship, and I hope you break every scoring record in the books." Only one of McGuire's wishes was to be fulfilled.

The new coach began making changes in the team immediately. He installed a fast-breaking college style offense that was keyed to the talents of the Warrior backcourt men, Guy Rodgers and Al Attles. He moved Tom Gola, a five year veteran at guard, up to forward to help Wilt in rebounding. The team had been strengthened with the acquisition of Tom Meschery, a 6 feet 6 inch rookie forward, and a fine one.

McGuire also sought to make changes in Wilt's style of play—changes that would fit the new Warrior tactics.

He wanted Wilt to feed the ball more into the other player so as to keep the defense alert. When Chamberlain did shoot, he wanted him to rely less on his fall-away shot. Instead, he wanted Wilt to "go for the basket," that is, to break for a rebound position under the boards following his shot.

The amiable coach was high in his praise of his towering charge. "You know, Wilt," he said, "every team in the league plays hardest against us because of you. It's a very great compliment to you."

In press interviews he seldom failed to characterize Wilt as anything but "the greatest." "And he will get even greater," McGuire said.

By the end of the exhibition season a warm rapport existed between Wilt and his new coach. It was obvious that Wilt liked and respected McGuire. It was reflected in his play. He was shooting more accurately, rebounding higher and playing a more effective role in the team's defense than he ever had before. Foul shots were no longer his great bugaboo, though they were still something of a problem.

When the season opened, the team was happy and spirited. The McGuire magic had worked.

In spite of their high morale, the team sputtered from the start. They would win one game and then lose the next, and as early as the third week of the season they were lodged behind the Celtics and ahead of the Nationals in the familiar surroundings of second place.

A word about the Celts is necessary at this juncture. Before the 1961–1962 season opened, the team was something of a question mark. Bill Sharman, who had averaged 16.3 points a game was gone; so was Gene Conley, their substitute center. But the previous season's Most Valuable Player, Bill Russell, was back, and so was Bob Cousy. Cousy, however, was 33 now and observers felt it was about time he began slowing down.

Any doubts about the Celtics were removed at once, for from the opening game they ran roughshod over every team in the league. They boasted a sound defense, and on attack, a matchless balance, with five or six men hitting 20 points or more every game. By late December they had lost only three games of the 26 they had played (the Warriors had not been able to beat them once), and it seemed the only thing that could slow them down would be the break for the All Star game.

The Warriors meanwhile were deepening the crinkles in McGuire's face and adding gray to his red wavy hair.

They were not getting the speed, fire or feeding support from Al Attles and Guy Rodgers that had been expected. The years were beginning to show on Paul Arizin, and Tom Gola had been hampered by injuries. Rookie Tom Meschery was a bright spot, but he couldn't make up for the inadequacies elsewhere. What the team needed most was a battler, a driving, scrambling player like Boston's Tommy Heinsohn who could ignite the team.

The responsibility for the success of the team fell almost exclusively upon Wilt's broad and well-muscled shoulders, and he responded in a manner that was seldom short of spectacular.

Recall, Wilt in his rookie year had averaged 37.6 points per game. The following year he averaged 38.3. Under McGuire's ministrations, Chamberlain exploded. After the first 32 games of the season, he was averaging 48.5 points a game. In 17 of those games, Wilt had drilled home 50 points or more (and Philadelphia had won 13 of these 17).

In addition to hitting field goals by the dozens, he was showing remarkable success from the foul line. His average in that department stood at .578, and while not particularly good when compared to that of other players in the NBA, it was downright lofty by Wiltonian standards.

In one fantastic streak midway in the season, Wilt

had point totals of 78, 61, 55, 54, 52, 43, 50, 57 and 55. "That's more than some players get in a whole career," remarked Tom Gola.

The 78 points, an all-time league record, came in a triple overtime game against the Los Angeles Lakers at Convention Hall. Early in January, in regulation time, Wilt hit 73 points against the Chicago Packers, the league's newest entry.

But Chamberlain's most phenomenal showing came towards the end of the season in a game played at Hershey. On the night of March 2, in one awesome swoop, he made a shambles of almost every league scoring record.

The Knicks, mired in last place in the league, were the unfortunate sufferers.

From the game's beginning, Wilt was hitting with every kind of shot—with dunks and on conventional lay-ups but he relied on his favorite weapon, his lovely fall-away, most often. His teammates realized he was having an unstoppable night and fed the ball in to him at every opportunity. At the end of the first quarter he had 23 points, and the Warriors had a frightening 42–26 lead.

What Wilt had fired up was his wondrous success at the foul line. In the first quarter he had an incredible 9 for 9.

Richie Guerin was hitting for the Knickerbockers and by halftime New York had closed the gap some, drawing within 11 points, 79–68. But by this time, the crowd of 4,124 had all its attention focused on Chamberlain. He had accrued 41 points by the halftime break and a new individual scoring record seemed very possible. When the teams returned for the third quarter, Wilt's every move was cheered.

Wilt continued to pour in points and the game turned into a frenzied burlesque of the sport. The Knicks were in no mood to be victimized by Chamberlain, but they were unable to stop him, even by mobbing him with three or four defenders, so they resorted to slow-down tactics, holding the ball for a full 24 seconds every time they got possession.

Early in the fourth quarter, Wilt broke his regulation game record of 73 points to the accompaniment of ecstatic screams from the fans, hundreds upon hundreds of whom had left their seats and now ringed the court. A few moments later, Wilt burst through the 78 point barrier, the triple-overtime record he had established a few months before.

The court became a frantic melee. The Knicks would foul every Warrior but Wilt in an effort to gain possession, and when the Knicks were in control, the Warriors would purposely foul.

Wilt's point total zoomed into the high 80's, but the crowd wanted more. If any member of the Warriors attempted a shot, he was soundly booed. Whenever Philadelphia got the ball, the crowd would scream, "Give it to Wilt! Give it to Wilt!"

The final minutes of the game were a kind of delirium to the fans and the players. Wilt hit 94, then 96, then 98—and with each basket the mob scene grew wilder.

With only 46 seconds to play, Wilt got possession near the Knicks' basket, and he bounded high in the air, and jammed in a beautiful dunker, the one-hundredth point. As the ball swished through the cords, all semblance of sanity vanished and the crowd poured out on to the court.

They mobbed about Chamberlain, shaking his hands and clapping him on the back. The game was delayed for several minutes while police sought to clear the floor.

When the final buzzer came, the fans swarmed out again to besiege Wilt. He floundered about in the mob like a ship in an angry sea until police were able to clear a path to the Warrior dressing room.

Chamberlain's 100 point total ranks as one of basketball's most monumental personal achievements. In the whole history of the sport, only three times before had one player recorded 100 points in a game, and never had it happened in the pro ranks.

Three college players had turned the trick: Frank Selvy of Furman University, Paul Arizin of Villanova University and Bevo Francis of Rio Grande. Only Selvy's "century," scored against Newberry in 1954, is recognized by the National Collegiate Association. The other players scored theirs against junior college competition.

The final score saw the Warriors on top—naturally —169–147. The total points scored, 316, set a new league record.

Wilt came out of the game with a fistful of other league marks to his credit besides the 100 point single game scoring record. The effort set a new record for points by a player in one half (59), for most points in one quarter (31), for the most free throws attempted (32) and for the most free throws made (28).

"I wasn't even thinking of hitting 100," Wilt said after the game. "But after putting in nine straight free throws, I was thinking about a foul shooting record."

Wilt declared it was his greatest game. Nobody disagreed.

In the National Basketball Association's Official Guide, Wilt's tremendous feat looks like this:

Chamberlain's Scoring by Periods

Quarter	Field Goals		Fouls	
	Attempted	Made	Attempted	Made
1st	14	7	9	9
2nd	12	7	5	4
3rd	16	10	8	8
4th	21	12	10	7
Totals	63	36	32	28

Quarter	Rebounds	Assists	Pf	Points
1st	10	0	0	23
2nd	4	1	1	18
3rd	6	1	0	28
4th	5	0	1	31
Totals	25	2	2	100

In the years that followed that evening in March 1962 on the Hershey court, neither Wilt himself nor any other player in the NBA has come close to equaling 100 points. Chances are no one ever will. It looms as one of those super-records that will stand for decades and very possibly for all time.

The nearest Wilt has come was 73 points that he scored against the Knicks in November 1962.

Of the other players in the league, Oscar Robertson, with a 56 point total netted in a game during the 1964–1965 season, has mustered the most serious threat, though an accumulation of a mere 56 points can scarcely be termed a "threat."

When the season was over and the league statisticians handed in their accounts, it was found that Wilt had rewritten the record books. He became the first player in the history of the league to score 4,000 points in a single season. His final total was 4,029, which gave him a season average of a colossal 50.4 points per game.

Wilt eclipsed a gaggle of other records that year. These included: most field goals attempted (3,159), most field goals made (1,597), most free throws attempted (1,362), most free throws made (835), most minutes played (3,882), most games scoring 50 or more points (44) and, to his chagrin, most fouls missed in one season (528).

Late in the season, Philadelphia made a determined drive to catch the runaway Celtics, but Boston's early speed had put them out of reach. They finished first, and the Warriors second.

However, on the basis of their late season play, Philadelphia was given an excellent chance to unseat the Celtics in the playoffs, and as the team headed for Syracuse for the opening of the semi-finals, McGuire's charges were filled with optimism.

17

"No One Knows Your Name"

IN THE FIRST TWO GAMES against Syracuse, the Warriors played in typically Frank McGuire fashion. They were determined and deliberate and stressed defensive tactics every inch of the way. Wilt blocked shots, ruled the boards and from the pivot passed off to Arizin and Meschery, who together led the way in scoring. The Warriors won both games.

They tried to clinch the series using the same strategy but the Nationals were on to them by now and managed to squeeze out a 101–100 victory.

McGuire was disgruntled at losing. He called the plane flight to Syracuse for the fourth game, "the most totally unnecessary trip ever taken." The team, too, was dispirited and having to share the aircraft with the winning Syracuse players did not help their morale. They lost in Syracuse and the playoff was knotted at 2–2.

There was a day off before the deciding game at

Convention Hall, and the rest proved to be the medicine the Warriors needed. They whipped the Nationals 121–104 with Wilt hitting for 56 points, a new playoff record.

The very next night the division finals opened in Boston, the sixth game in eight days for the weary Warriors. On the other hand, the Celtics had been resting in Boston for a week and one-half. Boston's Red Auerbach, fearing that his Celts might lack in shooting accuracy because of their layoff, had the team stress defensive tactics. The strategy was successful beyond his dreams as the Celtics held the Warriors to an infinitesimal 35 points for the first half. It was an easy win for the Bostonians.

The second game, in Philadelphia, was a thriller. Several times the Warriors seemed headed for defeat, but they never gave up. With 10 minutes remaining, Philadelphia was 10 points behind. With six minutes left, they were 7 behind. With four minutes left, they had closed the gap to 2.

Then Wilt, who had shown well throughout the game, turned the tide in Philadelphia's favor with a brilliant burst of pressure play. York Larese missed an outside jumper and Wilt, following the shot, stuffed it in with one hand to tie the score.

Then, like an outsized gazelle, he wheeled and raced to the other end of the court, just in the nick of time to block Tommy Heinsohn's attempted lay-up. Heinsohn tried again, was fouled and made one shot.

With the Celtics now ahead again, 103–102, Wilt pounded to the other end of the court. Meschery missed a jumper, and as it came off the rim, Wilt bounded basket high and his long fingers flipped it through. Now the Warriors were ahead—and they stayed ahead.

Philadelphia lost the third game of the series, which was played in Boston, but they won the fourth game before the friendly fans at Convention Hall. The contest saw Wilt get Russell in foul trouble in the first quarter and the Boston strong man's effectiveness was thereby diminished.

With the series now tied again, the Warriors emplaned to Boston for the fifth game. It was not much of a game, but it has become memorable in that it featured more sensational brawling than anything Boston had seen since the Battle of Bunker Hill.

About the game itself—it was over early. The Celtics sprang to a 10–2 lead and stretched it to 10 points at the end of the first quarter. They led 72–49 at the half. That was the game. For the record, the score saw Boston on top, 119–104.

The fireworks came in the fourth quarter. Early in the period, Wilt collided with Sam Jones, the Celtics 6 feet 4 inch guard. Immediately an angry argument flared between them. Jones started to back away from Chamberlain, but Wilt grabbed him by the wrist.

"Let me go!" Jones yelled. With that he broke from Wilt's hold, dashed off the court, scooped up a vacant ball boy's stool, and swung it threateningly at the now bewildered Chamberlain. (Explained Jones after the game: "I thought he was gonna swing at me, so I ran and grabbed the stool for protection. He weighs 260 pounds, you know.")

Immediately referees, policemen, ushers and other players rushed forth to separate the two combatants. Even Boston fans flooded onto the court.

Order was restored, but not for long. Before another point was scored, Guy Rodgers fired a left hook to the mouth of the unsuspecting Carl Braun. It landed nicely, and another mob scene quickly ensued. ("I thought Braun was going to hit me, so I slugged him first," said Rodgers in *his* post fight interview.)

Play resumed again, but less than a minute later,

Rodgers, when threatened by Boston's Jim Loscutoff, went for the same stool Jones had sought to use. The Boston fans screamed at Rodgers and one of them dashed out onto the court after the stocky Warrior playmaker. This fan and several others were quickly ejected.

Later in the quarter, Tommy Heinsohn flung a shoulder at Philadelphia's Ted Luckenbill and for this he was banished from the scene.

Not once during these several clashes did the referees call a foul. The next day, however, five of the warring players were fined $50 each.

Though he was not fined, and though he was not struck by any blow, Wilt may have suffered the most from the battling in Boston. During his brief clash with Jones, an alert press photographer had snapped a picture and it showed Chamberlain's massive form bearing down in menacing fashion upon a smaller adversary. It made Wilt look like a bully intent upon intimidation. Jones, his face to camera and a look of terror upon it, was shown reaching for the stool. The photograph was serviced by a press association and it appeared in newspapers across the country.

Two days later, in the more tranquil surroundings of Convention Hall, the Warriors evened the series for the third time. They took the lead early and never faltered. The game was played before the largest home-town crowd of the season and a few members of the throng brandished small footstools for the players to see. After a day's rest, the team left for Boston and the showdown game. Despite the fact that the Celtics were favored by 11 points, the Warrior team was deeply confident. "We need a great effort to beat them at home," McGuire said, "but I think we can do it."

It was a thrill-packed game that seesawed back and forth from the opening jump, and came down to the very last minute with the Celtics holding a slight edge. Then Wilt engineered a three-point play that produced a tie, 107–107. There were only 16 seconds left.

Boston worked the ball down court in their attempt to set up a final score, but the Warriors defended like demons and the seconds ticked away without the Celtics being able to get a shot off. Then at the last possible moment, K. C. Jones leaped high in the air to fire a pass to Sam Jones in the keyhole. Sam jumped and shot. The ball never touched the rim; it was perfect.

Instantly the Warriors called time out to stop the clock. Disheartened by Jones' last ditch effort that had put the Celtics ahead, the Warriors were further crushed when they looked at the clock. There was one second remaining.

In a final desperation play, Ed Conlin, in for Guy Rodgers who had fouled out, looped a long and arcing pass to Wilt who was positioned under the Boston basket. ("Everyone knew what we were trying to do," recalls Conlin. "Wilt looked like he was surrounded by an army.") Chamberlain got a hand on the ball but Russell batted it away and with it went the Warriors' chances. Then came the strident bawl of the buzzer. The game was over. The season was over.

The Warriors were hailed far and wide for their fine showing against the Celtics, for no team in recent years had come so close to beating the champions.

But Frank McGuire summed up best the feeling of Wilt and the other Warriors when he said, "In this country when you finish second no one knows your name."

18

The Critics

WILT WAS KEENLY DISAPPOINTED at his team's failure on the playoffs; but as bad as losing—perhaps even worse—was the mounting criticism being leveled at him by fans, newspaper reporters and rival players. Instead of being applauded for his outstanding role in bringing the Warriors to a second place finish, Wilt heard himself being blamed as the person responsible for his team's failure to win the Eastern Division title.

The most common criticism was that Wilt was not a team player, and the faultfinders pointed to the passel of personal scoring records he had accrued over the year as proof of their charge.

Indeed, sometimes after Wilt had scored 50 or even 60 points a game, and his team had lost, he was censured for being too much of an individual star. But if he didn't score a bundle of points, he was blamed, too. "Whatever Wilt does is at once too much and not enough," said Arthur Daley in the New York *Times*.

Wilt declared he was "sick and tired" of such charges. "It's like someone telling Roger Maris if he hits homers for the Yankees it doesn't help them, but if he doesn't hit homers he's a bum."

Wilt was frowned upon because he did not play defense with the aggressiveness of Bill Russell, shoot with the versatility of Elgin Baylor or set up plays and pass the way Bob Cousy could.

Actually, to criticize a player who can average more than 50 points and 25 rebounds a game is somewhat foolish. It is like criticizing Babe Ruth because he didn't steal bases.

It calls to mind the statement Illinois football coach Bob Zuppke made when Red Grange was tearing up the nation's gridirons for the Illini. "All Grange can do is run," an observer remarked. "Yeah," answered the coach. "And all Galli-Curci can do is sing."

"The trouble is," says one of Wilt's former teammates, "Wilt is so close to perfection, he's always being compared to the perfect. If he did everything better than anyone else, someone would say something like, 'He's all right, but he doesn't have a very good shot with his right foot.' "

During the season, Frank McGuire would have no part in the stream of disapproval aimed at Wilt. Rather than attempt to have Wilt pass more and shoot less, McGuire was Wilt's No. 1 cheerleader as the records fell. The coach would leap to Wilt's defense when the big man was assailed by a newspaperman.

It was charged that Wilt seldom played a game in which he gave his best 100 percent of the time. This charge stirred him to anger.

"Who does?" he asked. "You have to pace yourself in this game. You have to have something left at the end."

Wilt explains that playing in the NBA is a great deal different than playing for a college team. "In college you play only 19 or 20 games a year. You can go full blast and rest the next day. But it's not like that in the pros. Sometimes you play five days in a row in five different cities. After the game there's a plane trip. If you let it, the schedule can burn you out."

There were glaring inconsistencies in many of the critical remarks aimed at Wilt. When he first came into the league, fans rebuked him for his dunk shot. "All he can do is stand there and stuff the ball into the basket," was a typical remark.

So Wilt worked hard to perfect his fall-away shot. When he became proficient in its use, the critics chirped, "Wilt shouldn't fade-away from the basket like that; he's out of position for the rebound."

And the times Wilt has concentrated on defense, he has heard himself accused of playing at one end of the court. "But if I rush around like mad to the other end of the court, they say I'm hogging all the action. Man, I can't win!"

When the Warriors were defeated by the Celtics in the Eastern Division finals, Wilt heard it said that no team on which he had performed had ever won a championship. He was an All America choice at the University of Kansas for two years, yet the Jayhawks never won the NCAA title. And now, over three seasons with the professionals, no team on which he had played had been able to win the NBA title.

Can one man give a team a championship? It is not likely.

Ty Cobb, in a major league career that spanned more than two decades, and in which he achieved heights unequaled by a player before or since, never competed in a World Series. Jimmy Brown, the magnificent fullback for the Cleveland Browns, smashed league rushing records for seven years before his team won a championship. Oscar Robertson of the Cincinnati Royals, superlative on both offense and defense, has never been on a championship team. There are scores of other examples. Great athletes—super athletes, if you will—do not necessarily make for championship teams.

It was always Wilt's contention during these early days as a professional that the Warriors had the misfortune to be playing in the Eastern Division of the NBA with the Celtics, a team he often described as "the best in the world."

"Maybe we don't have the players to cope with them," he said to Milt Gross of the New York *Post,* "but what team in the league has?"

Wilt, not yet 26, could not get used to being called names like "the lone gunner." A NBA referee charged, "If Chamberlain were six inches shorter, you wouldn't know about him." A newspaper reporter declared Wilt was becoming "the most famous also-ran in the history of sport."

The words hurt Wilt. He came to realize the only way he could stop such slander would be to lead his team to a championship. Now he wanted the title more than he ever had before.

19

Pulling a Switch

BEGINNING EARLY in 1962 and through the final stages of the season when the playoff games were being contested, rumors were rife that the Philadelphia franchise was to be, as they say, "switched"—moved to another city. In this case, San Francisco.

In the National Basketball Association teams are constantly being added, subtracted or moved about. If the Philadelphia switch were to become a reality, it would merely be another move of the same type of the 30 or so that had preceded it since the league was formed in 1946.

Why move the Philadelphia franchise? Owner Eddie Gottlieb had two reasons, both of them extremely valid ones.

Foremost was money. As Gottlieb described the offer that had been made to him, it was a "once in a lifetime" opportunity. Then in his early sixties, Gottlieb, or "Gotty" as his friends called him, had organized, coached and owned the team since the days a hot dog sold for a dime.

In 1946 he had become General Manager and Coach of the Warrior team. Five years later he bought the franchise. He paid a reported $25,000 for it. Now he was being offered $850,000 for the property. Such opportunities are, indeed, of a once in a lifetime nature.

The other reason for selling concerned Wilt. While huge crowds had packed Convention Hall to stare at Chamberlain in popeyed awe during his first year with the Warriors, in the seasons that followed attendance showed a steady decline. Gottlieb reported sadly that aside from the playoff games, there had only been one sellout in the season just finished.

What had happened was that Wilt had made what always before had been extraordinary—the ability to score 50 points or more a game—quite commonplace. Wilt had become too successful in his trade. Who would pay to see a quarterback pass for a touchdown every time he got his hands on the ball, or a boxer always win by a first round knockout?

With the diminishing attendance, Wilt's large salary and that of Frank McGuire became a hefty load for Gotty to bear. He declared that in spite of the fact the team had played well and had made the playoffs, the Warriors had lost money for the year.

For a time it appeared that the NBA's Board of Governors would not give permission for the franchise to be transferred, but at length approval was granted, and now San Francisco had Wilt and the Warriors and Philadelphia did not.

By moving to San Francisco, the Warriors became members of the NBA's Western Division, and no more would they have to duel the unconquerable Celtics for the division championship.

However, in the West a new basketball power, as

formidable as the Celtics, was said to be rising—the
Los Angeles Lakers. The Lakers had won the Western
Division title the previous year and easily, and for the
season ahead, they looked to be greatly strengthened.
Elgin Baylor was returning from Army duty. Baylor,
second only to Wilt as a scorer, and as fine an all
around player as the league could boast, was the "one"
of the Los Angeles one-two punch. The "two" was
guard Jerry West, whose size, speed and reach made
him a standout in the backcourt, and whose shooter's
eye made him a constant scoring threat.

The Lakers also had the very able Rudy LaRusso at
forward, and Frank Selvy and Hot Rod Hundley at
guard. On the basis of this talent, and the way that
talent had performed in pre-season exhibition games,
the Lakers were rated every bit the equal of the Celtics. So despite the fact the Warriors had left the
Celtics behind in the Eastern Division, the struggle to
win a division championship was not going to be any
easier for them.

But the first team to give the Warriors trouble that
year was not the Lakers, but the Giants—the San Francisco baseball Giants, that is.

Recall that the year 1962 was the year in which the
San Francisco Giants won the National League pennant
and were to meet the New York Yankees in the World
Series. The city went absolutely wild over baseball. In
October, when the sports fans and the press might well
have been paying some heed to the Warriors, the World
Series occupied everyone's attention. Unfortunately
for the Warriors, the series was lengthened by additional days required for coast-to-coast travel, and by
postponements because of rain, and all the while the
Giants held the spotlight. So much did baseball dominate the scene that when Wilt's name finally did break
into the news columns, he was referred to as "the Willie
Mays of pro basketball."

It did not help matters that the Warriors did not play an exhibition game in their new hometown. Their schedule, a punishing one, took them from the Ozark Mountains to the state of Hawaii, but San Francisco never made the itinerary.

One wag thought it would be fitting to dub the team the "San Francisco Strangers." That's how bad things were.

Late in October, a few days before the Warriors' opening game, the team's players, coaches and officials took part in a motorcade up San Francisco's main thoroughfare, Market Street, and on to City Hall where Wilt, representing the team, was to be presented with the keys of the city.

But the fete was confused with a similar greeting that had been planned for the Giants, and many of the San Franciscans who lined the streets thought the open convertibles contained baseball stars.

"Which one is Mays?" a youngster wanted to know.

"Rodgers?" asked a man when a car containing Guy Rodgers passed by. "What's he doing here? I thought we traded André Rodgers to the White Sox."

On the steps of City Hall, Wilt's unmistakable form quickly dispelled the confusion. "That's Wilt the Stilt," a woman exclaimed when she saw Chamberlain step over and out of the open car without even bothering to open the door.

The competition with baseball was bad enough, but it did not help matters any that on the evening the Warriors were to premiere at the Cow Palace, their home court in San Francisco, the team had to compete with the Gene Fullmer-Dick Tiger middleweight chamionship which was held at Candlestick Park.

With the citizenry so preoccupied with other sports attractions, the Warriors debut was marred by a slim turnout. Slightly more than 5,000 San Franciscans were on hand.

With Wilt leading the way, the Warriors won their opener. They then won the next two before losing in overtime to Cincinnati, and their brief burst took them to the top of the league as the Lakers faltered.

In one of these early season games, Wilt scored the 10,000th point of his career. The Cow Palace was the scene; the Knicks were the opposition.

The Warriors clung to first place until the second week in November. Then one evening in Los Angeles they faced the Lakers who beat them conclusively and knocked them from their high perch. The fact that the Warriors lost was not really important (for they were to lose many more games than they were to win that season), but the pattern they followed in losing was significant.

"Let's face it," Wilt said before the game. "We don't have anyone who can guard Baylor and we don't have anyone who can guard West. But they don't have anyone who can guard me." It was to prove an accurate estimate of the situation, indeed, of the whole season.

From the start Wilt had the Los Angeles fans rolling in the aisles. He hit from every angle and with every type of shot. In the first quarter he scored 23 points while his teammates chipped in with four others to give the Warriors a 27–25 edge.

Wilt continued on his scoring rampage but the Warrior supporting cast seldom helped. They could not hit with their outside shots and were clearly not the equal of the Lakers on rebounds.

Meanwhile, Jerry West and Elgin Baylor were—to-gether—matching Wilt's point production. In the last 15 minutes, the Warrior defenses cracked completely and West hit the basket as if it were an open manhole. He ended with 49 points. Baylor gathered 30.

Wilt? Wilt had 72. Unfortunately, only two other Warriors hit double figures, and San Francisco forwards contributed a mere 14 points to the effort so Wilt's 72 point effort was in a losing cause. As a matter of fact, the Laker win was earned without too much difficulty. The final score was 127–115.

The game was very typical of many that were to follow. Wilt ran up 59 points and the Warriors lost to Cincinnati. The next game he scored 61 against the Royals, but it didn't change the outcome. He blasted 53 and later 63 in games against the Lakers, but both times the Warriors were beaten.

It had to happen. The Warriors fell into a dreadful slump and proceeded to lose 11 games in a row, a streak that skidded them to the very bottom of the league's standings.

Bob Feerick, the San Francisco coach (Frank McGuire had taken a coaching position at the University of South Carolina and did not move West with the team), who had been eminently successful at the University of Santa Clara for more than a decade, was having his worst suspicions about the team confirmed. Guy Rodgers, Al Attles and Tom Gola were superior backcourt men, but neither could hit consistently with an outside shot.

The situation was worsened by the fact that the team did not have first rate forecourt men. Paul Arizin had retired the previous season, and Tom Meschery had cracked a bone in his left wrist and was on the injured list as a result. The Warrior rookies had proved to be a disappointment.

San Francisco was a one man team and the opposition played them that way. The key to winning against the Warriors was stopping Wilt. More than ever he was shoved and mauled and his rib cage became the league punchboard.

Help, however, did come when, in the midst of the team's losing streak, the Warriors completed a player swap with the Knickerbockers that brought Ken Sears and Willie Naulls to San Francisco in exchange for Tom Gola. Sears and Naulls were expected to team the outside shooting support they so desperately needed and thereby relieve the fierce pressure on Chamberlain.

For a time the team improved, and even put together a modest winning streak. But after the midseason hiatus for the All Star game, the Warriors started to lose again with their early season consistency.

Losing more than winning is bad enough, but for Wilt the season had other moments of misery.

One came in St. Louis in a game against the Hawks. Wilt was ejected from a game for the first time in his career. Referee Red Oates, then in his rookie year, dismissed Chamberlain in the first quarter of play for what he called "unsportsmanlike conduct."

Wilt had protested what Coach Feerick later described as a "terrible call" against rookie Wayne Hightower. So Oates called a technical on Wilt. When Wilt continued to protest, Oates hit him with a second tecnical. Under NBA rules two technicals bring automatic ejection.

Feerick felt Oates acted rashly. "The two technicals came only five seconds apart," Feerick said. "I don't think any experienced official in the league would have called it that way."

A few days later Wilt established another first for himself when he became involved in a heated slugging match. Bob Ferry, the 6 feet 8 inch center with the Detroit Pistons, was the "almost" victim.

The brawl took place at the Cow Palace and was touched off when Ferry and Guy Rodgers, a mere 6 footer, scuffled for the ball. Ferry fired an elbow or two and Rodgers answered back with his fists. Then Wilt charged into the fray to aid Rodgers. Players from both teams streamed onto the court to separate the contestants.

The referee called a held ball and the players walked to the center of the court for a jump. As they did, Ferry turned and said something to Wilt. Precisely what he said never was recorded, but Wilt's answer was a straight right hand. Ferry ducked—surely his best move of the night. Quickly the officials intervened.

The season saw another piece of sad business enacted when the players of the NBA selected the league All Star teams. Each year two teams are chosen, one from the Eastern Division and one from the Western, and then the two teams meet in the mid-season All Star game.

At the time the ballots were cast, Wilt was the league's leading scorer and rebounder, yet he was not voted a member of the Western squad. Some of the players, unfortunately, had let their resentment for Wilt and his talents interfere with their good judgment. Not so much for Wilt, but for professional basketball, in general, it was a humilating experience. It had never happened before; it has never happened since.

By mid-season, Los Angeles had built an eight game lead over second place St. Louis, but the Warriors were not concerned about catching the Lakers or the Hawks. Mired in last place, San Francisco's quarry was the Detroit Pistons who were immediately ahead of them in the league standings.

For the Warriors the season turned on a final road trip in March, a crucial four games in four different cities that were to decide whether they or the Pistons would win the all-important third place playoff berth. It was a grim trip.

The first of the four games were played in New York and here the Warriors renewed their fistic rivalry with the Pistons in the first game of a double-header at Madison Square Garden. Fans who saw the game do not remember who won or lost. What they do remember was the furious player free-for-all that turned the contest into a court version of the Donnybrook Fair.

Again Bob Ferry was in the center of things. In the final seconds of the third quarter, the Warriors' Al Attles, for reasons never made clear, tackled Ferry. Immediately the battle was joined, with Ferry and Attles the principals. Players from both benches rushed into the melee, some to throw punches, some to act as peacemakers.

Wilt took a peacemaker role. Fights had broken out in several places on the court and Wilt waded into several of them. To rescue Wayne Hightower, he shoved 7 foot Walter Dukes into a group of gaping spectators. He tossed Detroit's Bailey Howell halfway across the court. Finally he managed to get where Ferry and Attles were battling. Attles was on the floor, and Wilt picked him up as easily as one might pick up a small puppy.

The brawl was declared a draw, but the game wasn't. When play resumed, the Pistons spurted for 20 points while the Warriors were scoring only 5 and the burst carried the Detroiters to victory.

In Baltimore the very next night, things got even more bizarre. The Warriors were locked in a close struggle with the Chicago Zephyrs when midway in the second quarter whistles blew, buzzers sounded and the public address announcer ordered the arena cleared of fans, players, officials—everyone. A telephoned message reported a bomb had been placed in the arena. Almost in disbelief of what was happening, the players went back to their hotel. The fans—almost 6,000 of them—milled about in the street.

The police and fire departments searched the premises, but nothing was found. Again the interruption in court action worked in the opposition's favor. When play resumed the Zephyrs exploded while the Warriors fizzled.

The Warriors hoped that the brawls and bomb scares

were behind when they met the Pistons two days later in what was the most fateful game of the season. Winning now was a must.

For a time the Warriors hopes were bright. They held a 9 point advantage with less than seven minutes to play, but the Pistons roared back to take the lead. Wilt, who scored a total of 51 points, sent the game into overtime with a field goal that knotted the count, 112-all. But in the overtime the Pistons prevailed, 131–123.

"We're dead," a disheartened Bob Feerick said after the game.

The crusher was delivered in Syracuse two nights later.

Wilt shot out the lights, hitting for 70 points, but the Warriors lost. The final score was 163–148. Obviously nobody played defense. Now the Warriors had fallen three full games in back of the Pistons and even though a mathematical chance remained that they could make the playoffs, the players knew the season was over.

Many observers were quick to place the blame for the team's terrible failure on Wilt.

The familiar criticisms were heard. Some nights Wilt was denounced for hogging the ball. Some nights he was accused of refusing to shoot even when in the clear. Some nights he was charged with doing both —but in different quarters.

Agreed, Mr. Chamberlain did have his moments of petulance. But the collapse of the Warrior team was due to reasons much more grievous.

Paul Arizin's decision not to come West with the Warriors hurt the team deeply. As a shooter, as a feeder and, most important, as a field general, his talents were sorely needed.

The trade that brought Naulls and Sears to San Francisco did not live up to expectations. For a time the new players did reduce the pressure upon Wilt, but by season's end Chamberlain was being as brutally harassed as he had at any time during the season.

The Warriors not only did poorly in the league standings, they flunked out at the box office, too. Attendance averaged less than 4,000 a game over the year, but many of these attendees were special one dollar admissions, granted late in the season when fans had developed a tendency to stay away from the Cow Palace in great throngs.

The Warriors ended the season at home by losing in overtime to the Lakers. In the daily newspapers, results of the game were buried with the soccer scores and bowling news. The sports pages were again ablaze with baseball, and the fact that the Giants had beaten the Red Sox in a pre-season exhibition game got the biggest play. The long and dreary season had come full circle.

20

A New Model

FOR THE 1963–1964 season, it was all too familiar.
Wilt had a new coach, his fourth in five seasons, and
the new coach was announcing plans to change Wilt's
style of play. By now Chamberlain knew the script
almost by heart.

Alex Hannum was the coach. Tall—6 feet 7 inches—
blue-eyed and balding and with a deserved reputation
as a referee baiter, Hannum had coached with notable
success at St. Louis and, most recently, at Syracuse.

After the close of the 1963 season, and following the
switch of the Syracuse franchise to Philadelphia, Hannum decided to retire. He moved to the West Coast
and planned to establish a construction business there,
but Eddie Gottlieb dangled a fancy offer in front of
him, and Hannum could not turn his back on it.

First, however, Hannum cleared the air on two matters.

"Does Wilt Chamberlain demand to play every minute of every game?" he asked Gottlieb.

To this Gotty answered a categorical "No."

"Is Wilt Chamberlain after points to insure his high salary?" was Hannum's other query.

Again Gottlieb answered "No," and it was just as unconditional.

The news that Hannum was to be the new Warrior coach made Wilt wince, for Hannum had long been one of Wilt's chief tormentors of the many and varied tormentors Wilt had in the NBA.

Whenever the Warriors played Syracuse, Wilt knew he was in for special harassment. NBA rules say a player cannot hold the ball in the keyhole for more than three seconds, so everytime Chamberlain got the ball under the Syracuse basket, Hannum would shriek, "Three seconds! Three seconds!" in an effort to unnerve Wilt. That is only one example; there are many others.

All the while Hannum was baiting Wilt from the bench, Dolf Schayes would make things difficult for Chamberlain on the floor. He would lean on Wilt like he was a fence post, or clutch his shirt or tug his belt. When Wilt plays basketball, it is normal for him to wear a pained expression. When his team played Syracuse, his expression was much more pained than usual.

At first there was hostility between Wilt and Hannum, but gradually Wilt responded to the plans that Hannum put forth to remodel the team. "Wilt is an uncoachable player," his critics have said of him. The experience with Hannum would prove otherwise.

The new coach set out to make profound alterations in the team, and Wilt loomed as one of Hannum's foremost targets. "Chamberlain cannot play for me the way he's played for other coaches. He has to change," Hannum said.

It has always been Wilt's contention that athletes cannot be changed very much in their style of play. It is always difficult to achieve, a little bit like teaching a dog to walk on its hind legs. It can be done, of course, but is the effect really worth it?

Most of the changes Hannum planned on instituting did not seem new to Wilt. Feeding was an example. Hannum urged Wilt to take on a more determined role as a feeder. Yet to Wilt there was nothing new about this. After Willie Naulls and Ken Sears had joined the Warriors the previous season, and Wilt had sharper shooters to pass to, he did indeed pass off. In fact, toward the end of the season he was earning six or seven assists a game, and only two players in the league averaged higher than that.

Hannum also wanted Wilt "to go to the basket more," a litany of Frank McGuire's. Taps and dunks were to be stressed so when shots were missed, by Wilt or others, Chamberlain would be in position for the rebound.

Such strategy Wilt claims isn't always successful. Sometimes it just isn't possible to get through the clogged middle and, overall, he feels he must constantly vary his style of offense to keep the defense alert. This meant, of course, there would be times that he would continue to rely on his fall away jumper.

Once Hannum's system was launched, people began to praise Wilt for his work on defense. Wilt shrugged off such plaudits. He felt he had always played a solid game on defense.

"I'm doing the same old stuff," he said to Leonard Lewin of the New York *Post* following a game at Madison Square Garden. "Defense is the one thing I did best since I was in high school."

Both Wilt and his coach had strong opinions, and both sets of opinions carried merit. Some lively arguments were the result.

In essence the changes that Hannum sought to make in his skyscraping center were not meant to produce a "new" Wilt Chamberlain. They were merely changes in emphasis.

Wilt accepted what Hannum was trying to do. "He is interested in winning; he buys what I say," Hannum declared. And he told Arnold Hano of *Sport* Magazine, "Wilt is one of the most cooperative players I've ever had."

The greatest and most substantial changes that Hannum wrought were upon the team as a whole.

In the first scrimmage of the pre-season training period, with Chamberlain absent from the scene, the new coach matched the previous season regulars against the rookies, and the rookies romped to an easygoing victory. Hannum was astonished. "The veterans were not capable of beating the rookies," he said. "They had forgotten how to play basketball. They had come to rely on Wilt so much they had forgotten they, too, had offensive and defensive responsibilities."

Hannum started rebuilding. In the scrimmages and over the entire exhibition season, he worked to make over the Warriors. Everybody on the floor moved. Everybody sought to get free for shots. Wilt was running, too, and passing and rebounding more than he ever had before. His scoring output shrank.

Hannum also worked on the team's psyche. Team spirit was high. On the bench Hannum was always the relentless "holler guy." "I feel enthusiasm is infectious," Hannum once said, "and it's my nature to be enthusiastic. If I wasn't enthusiastic I think it would affect my team in a negative way."

Change had also come to the Warriors in the person of rookie Nate Thurmond. At 6 feet 11 inches, Thurmond—he played college ball at Bowling Green University—could serve most teams in the NBA as a first string center, but with San Francisco he was to spell

Tom Meschery and Wayne Hightower at forward, and also serve as relief man for Wilt. In his five year career in the NBA, Wilt had never been so honored.

Late in September, after two weeks of training and scrimmages, the team left for Hawaii to open its exhibition season. The Philadelphia 76ers (the former Syracuse Nationals) and the Los Angeles Lakers were to provide the opposition in Hannum's unveiling of the new Warriors.

The change was startling to behold. The Warriors were running constantly, cutting for the basket or to corner openings for jump shots. On defense they really amazed, and Wilt was blocking shots and plucking rebounds from the defensive board with fierce energy.

Wilt was also scoring a great deal less. He was to average 21 points a game for the Hawaii exhibition contests (though he didn't play a full 48 minutes of every game), and 21 points was less than half his scoring average per game over the season before.

The crowds were frightfully small—one game attracted approximately 500 people—and one reason was because of the fans' disappointment in the new model Chamberlain. "Why isn't Wilt shooting?" a reporter asked, and Hannun explained he was changing the team's style of play.

The Hawaiians were unimpressed with the experiment, and with Wilt in general. Chamberlain finished a distant third to Hal Greer in the newsmen's balloting for the most valuable player of the tour.

When the team returned to the mainland, the experimentation continued. The exhibition schedule now took the Warriors through such byways as Missoula, Montana, Olympia, Washington, and Stockton, California, and some others, and at every stop their metamorphosis grew more firmly ingrained.

In pre-season estimates of the teams and the league, it was noted that the Warriors had finished next to the bottom of the league standings the year before, and most observers gave them very little chance to improve their ranking. But before the season was very old the Warriors showed the forecasters to be in serious error.

The league season opened in Baltimore against the Bullets (formerly the Chicago Zephyrs), and Wilt netted only 23 points, but the Warriors won, 103–102. The next night, in St. Louis, much the same thing happened. Wilt had a sparse 22 points, but the Warriors won again. This time the score was 99–95.

Hannum was enthusiastic about Wilt's performance in St. Louis. "He played an outstanding game, jamming the middle, blocking shots and guarding his man. He's doing everything we asked of him," the coach said.

Wilt's field goal output dwindled, not because he was missing shots, but simply because he was shooting less. In the year before he would have had as many as 40 field goal attempts in a game. Under Hannum's system he was averaging only about 20 tries a game.

His accuracy did not falter and he stood close to the .528 shooting percentage with which he had paced the league the year before. One night early in the season in a game against the Knicks in Boston, Wilt's precision as a gunner hit record heights.

Wilt's first attempt for a field goal missed, but it proved to be his only faulty shot of the night, as he connected with 18 consecutive shots before the Knicks could stop him. His brilliance broke a 12-year-old NBA record.

Wilt and Guy Rodgers broke the game wide open in the second quarter when Wilt scored 24 points, including 11 of his field goals. Rodgers, a feeding wizard, earned 11 assists for the quarter.

Despite their improved styling, Hannum was not expecting the team to perform any miracles—not right away, at any rate. He said that he would be happy if they played .500 ball over the first part of the season, and that was just about what they did, settling into third place not far behind Los Angeles and St. Louis but well ahead of fourth place Detroit.

The indication that better things were ahead came one evening in January when the Warriors met the Celtics at the Cow Palace. Though the season was not yet one-half complete, Boston had already made a shambles of the Eastern Division race by winning 25 of their first 30 games. The team was determined to get away fast to prove that Bob Cousy's retirement was not going to bother them, and their success in that aim surprised everyone including themselves. No Western Division team had been able to beat them.

From the opening tip-off the game was close and thrill-packed. With slightly less than three minutes remaining in the second quarter, Boston held a 46–42 lead. Then Wilt roared into action. He sank a foul toss, then dunked one and followed with a fade away jumper that didn't even touch the rim. Now San Francisco had the lead. Attles made it bigger with a long jumper just as the buzzer sounded. The Warriors were ahead, 49–46, when the teams filed to their dressing rooms.

The outcome turned on a single play late in the third quarter. Boston had fought back to take a slim lead, and just before the quarter ended Attles arced a long shot toward the basket. Wilt leapt so high you could have driven a Cadillac under his feet, and his fingers gently guided the ball into the basket. As Wilt came down he collided with Bill Russell and he sent the giant Boston center sprawling. It was several minutes before Russell gained his full equilibrium and while his head was clearing, Clyde Lovellette was shifted over to guard Wilt. Chamberlain's response to this piece of strategy was to drill three perfect jumpers over the outstretched arm of the bewildered Lovellette. With those six points as a nucleus, San Francisco built a 10 point lead, and from that point they were never headed.

A week later the Warriors jumped into second place, displacing St. Louis. Defense was the prime weapon in the game that saw the Warriors move ahead in the standings, an 89–79 defeat of Detroit. It was the lowest scoring game of the season. Also, it ranked as the fifth straight win for the San Franciscans, their longest streak since leaving Philadelphia two years before.

The Warriors' defensive skills were now being billed as the best in basketball, and this in a season where there was a definite emphasis on defense throughout the league. More times than not in the final stages of the league race, the San Franciscans were successful in holding the opposition to fewer than 100 points a game, a feat almost as notable as a pitcher hurling nine innings of shutout baseball.

Now from their second place plateau, the Warriors set out in chase of the league-leading Lakers. Early in February they caught them, and with hardly a pause bounded past and into the rarefied surroundings of first place. Except for brief early season glimpses, this was Wilt's first view from the top.

The Warriors took over first place in the standings by beating Baltimore in an overtime thriller. Field goals by Guy Rodgers and Gary Phillips gave the San Franciscans the lead in the extra period, and Wilt's block of a field goal attempt by Terry Dischinger with less than 10 seconds remaining preserved the team's two point advantage.

Through the remaining six weeks of the season, the Warriors fought to build their lead. They increased it to as much as three games, but in the final days it shrank as the St. Louis Hawks came on to challenge.

They surged past the Lakers, who were hit by injuries to both Baylor and West, and came within a single game of the Warriors.

And that was the way the teams ranked as the final day of the season arrived—the Warriors one game ahead of the Hawks. That evening in the gymnasium dressing room of the University of San Francisco (where some of their home games were played) there was a tense quietness as the Warriors pulled on their uniforms for a game against the Philadelphia 76ers. This was a must game for the Warriors, if there ever was one, for if they lost, and the Hawks beat the Pistons in Detroit, the standings would be tied and a playoff game would be required.

It would be good to be able to say that the Warriors finished the season in first place following a brilliant victory over the 76ers. They did finish first, but the end came rather undramatically. A few minutes before the San Franciscans went out onto the court to do battle with the 76ers, word was brought to them that the Hawks had lost.

In their jubilee, the players were quick to credit Alex Hannum. And Wilt, at a halftime meeting of the players, proclaimed Hannum as "the finest coach I ever played for." No one disagreed.

21

Boston Strong Man

IN THE WHOLE world of sport through the 1960's, no rivalry caught the public's imagination as did the year-in, year-out, head-to-head court clashes between Wilt and the magnificent center for the Boston Celtics, Bill Russell. Their first meeting in Wilt's rookie year, 1959, when Russell was beginning his fourth year in the league, had all the trappings of a crucial World Series game, and their scores of confrontations in basketball arenas across the country in the years that followed were seldom less exciting then the first one.

One of the rare bright spots for the Warriors in their first season in San Francisco came with the Celtics' first appearance at the Cow Palace. The personal duel between Russell, who had grown up in the Bay Area and had played high school and college ball there, attracted 12,067 fans, nearly double the home attendance of any previous Warrior game. The vast throng had little interest in the game itself or its outcome; they had come to watch the two giants do battle.

Russell is almost three years older than Wilt and about three inches shorter. He is slimmer and not as well muscled. In their early meetings, Russell had the edge in experience but, naturally, this advantage lessened as Wilt became wise in the ways of the pros. In later years, the advantage was on Wilt's side for Russell found it increasingly difficult to keep pace with his younger foe.

Russell first came to national attention when he led the University of San Francisco to 55 straight wins and two consecutive NCAA championships in 1955 and 1956.

Wilt was in high school at the time, but he had read all about Russell. Later, when Wilt was at the University of Kansas and making a western swing with the team, an occasional fan would point to Wilt and say, "There's Bill Russell." In Russell's hometown of San Francisco, Wilt was taken for Russell about half the time.

The confusion worked the other way. Early in 1956, Russell, then with the Celtics, visited Kansas City where Wilt was a local hero. "I'd sure like to meet that Chamberlain," Russell said. "People have been calling me 'Wilt the Stilt' since I got here."

Nowadays people seldom fail to distinguish between the two. Each is well known, and each has his own precise image.

Russell, of course, is basketball's defensive virtuoso. He consistently leads the league in rebounds, but his great value to the Celtics isn't revealed by statistical data. His hands are perhaps the most intimidating in all of basketball. They are everywhere, blocking shots and breaking up plays. Even more important, his very presence on the court is demoralizing to the opposition, and when facing him, a player finds it difficult not to be menaced out of shots.

"Actually," Russell has said, "I only block about five percent of the shots the opposition attempts. But my big advantage is that no one knows what five percent it's going to be."

Wilt has the greatest respect for Russell's professional abilities, though he feels that if Bill's career had been spent with a team less blessed with talent than the Celtics, Russell would have been a different type of player. With Boston, Russell had the opportunity to concentrate almost solely on defense. The Celtics had Tom Heinsohn, Frank Ramsey and Bill Sharman, and later, they had Sam Jones and John Havlicek, all of whom could put the ball into the basket while Russell was preventing the opposition from doing it.

Wilt felt that if Russell had played for the New York Knickerbockers, for example, he might never have become known as a defensive specialist, but would have had to produce as a scorer.

Wilt and Russell are close personal friends, but on the court they are bitter rivals, and their prime talents —Wilt's offensive brilliance and Russell's defensive prowess—burn the brightest when they face one another. In the NBA championship playoffs for 1963–1964, the jousting of these two court Goliaths would reach new heights.

In the Eastern Division finals, the Celtics rolled over the Cincinnati Royals with ease, trouncing them four games to one. In the West meanwhile, the Warriors downed the Hawks, but there was nothing simple about it.

One reason for San Francisco's difficulty with the Hawks was St. Louis' 6 feet 9 inch, 240 pound center, Zelmo Beaty. There were three centers in the league that gave Wilt consistent trouble. One was Russell, of course. Another was Cincinnati's Wayne Embry. The other was Zelmo Beaty.

The Warriors lost the first game of the series, a best four out of seven joust, squandering a 20 point lead by ball handling mistakes and an almost complete breakdown in outside point production. In the second game, like the first, played on the Warriors' home court, Wilt and Guy Rodgers starred as the team evened the series.

Then the action moved to St. Louis. Here the Hawks harassed Wilt from the front, the back, the sides—everywhere. There were times he looked as if he were trying to shoot or pass off from the center of the Chicago Bear line.

The fourth game, again in St. Louis, proved to be the key game. Despite the unsociable fans and the unfamiliar court, the Warriors won—the only game of the series they were to win on foreign territory. Back home, with Wilt hitting 50 points, they won again and went ahead in the series for the first time, three games to two.

Now it was back to St. Louis. There the Hawks evened things again.

Then the players clambered aboard their silvery shuttle for the flight to San Francisco, their fifth cross-country jaunt of the series. If the teams were less than nimble-footed when they arrived, no one could blame them.

Not only did the series come down to the final game, but to the final quarter.

In the waning minutes, the Warriors, who had been playing in low gear, suddenly became a team possessed. They broke into a wild scoring frenzy. Rodgers sank a free throw and then hit with a driving lay-up. He roared in for two more driving field goals and the crowd became hysterical.

Then Wilt's hand got hot. He stuffed one and followed with a pair of jumpers. Tom Meschery arced in a 20-footer, and Wilt capped the fierce drive with another stuffer. All this took place within three minutes, and it carried the Warriors to victory.

Now in his fifth season as a professional, Wilt looked forward anxiously to his first championship playoff series. He felt that the momentum the Warriors had gained in their final game with the Hawks would carry them to victory over the Celtics.

A few days before the series with the Bostonians was to open, Bill Russell announced he was considering retirement. He said he had been on the verge of a nervous breakdown all year, and disclosed he was bothered by arthritic knees and insomnia.

"Bill's a proud man," said Wilt. "Maybe he doesn't want to get past his peak before he quits."

But in the first game of the series, Russell gave not the slightest indication he was ready for either Social Security or Medicare.

Any Warrior who tried to drive the lane against Russell saw his shots blocked surely. Often he stole the ball. He subjected Wilt to unrelenting harassment and in the second and third periods, Wilt's total production was two points.

Actually the Warriors lost the game as early as the second quarter. The Celts opened with their defensive team, K. C. Jones, Tom Sanders and Russell. In the second quarter, Auerbach turned to his offensive power, with Frank Ramsey and John Havlicek keynoting the attack. They broke the game open and the demoralized Warriors weren't even able to make it close.

After the game Russell said it was obvious to him that Wilt was tired from the long and rugged series with the Hawks. Wilt agreed.

But he looked forward to the upcoming game. "I like to play Russell in back-to-back games," he said. "I'm always stronger than Bill the second night."

Wilt *was* the stronger of the two the second night.

His rebounding was superb and he was able to hit well with his fall away jumper. In total he gathered 32 points, including 14 field goals.

But a perennial Warrior failing bedeviled the team. They could not connect from the outside. As a result, the Celtics sagged off on Wilt, clogging the middle and nullifying Chamberlain's effectiveness in the pivot.

K. C. Jones pestered Wilt constantly and Russell never stopped trying to push him out of position.

All the while the Celts' front-line shooters, fed on Russell's pinpoint passes, were building the score. By the end of the third quarter, the Boston advantage had mounted to 30 points, 98–68, and that was about the story of the second game.

The game was on ice at that point, of course, but the action wasn't over.

Clyde Lovellette was inserted in the line-up in the final quarter in place of Russell. Immediately big Clyde took up Russell's role in grabbing at Wilt to harass him, or shoving him out of his position in the pivot. Suddenly the two men were jaw to jaw and angry words poured forth. Lovellette, rather tentatively, sought to push Wilt away.

With that Wilt uncorked a right hand, looping it at about half-speed to Lovellette's mouth. Lovellette was an enormous man, tall, stocky, and well-deserving of his nickname, "The Great White Whale." When the punch landed, he stood motionless for a second and then plopped into a sitting position on the floor, falling like a great sack of wet wash.

The Boston fans, seldom less than fanatical, now turned violent. Red Auerbach leaped from his seat on the bench to rage at Wilt. Then the referee called a personal foul on Lovellette but none on Chamberlain.

The fans and Auerbach were stunned, but only for an instant. Boos and catcalls all but lifted the Garden's roof. Auerbach turned livid and shrieked abuse in every direction and probably would be screaming yet, if Russell had not pulled him to the bench to still him.

Of course, the important fact was that the Warriors had lost and were now down two games to none. Proceedings moved to San Francisco.

Back among friends Hannum decried Boston's home court tactics. He protested that the officials looked the other way whenever Russell attempted to shove Wilt out of position, "How can we operate when our pivot man is being pushed?" he asked. He vowed that his "hustle and muscle team" would retaliate.

With the opening tip-off, it was obvious a remarkable change had come over the Warriors. Their outside shots were dropping with incredible consistency, and the team rushed to a 26–7 lead. Wilt, with 35 points, outplayed Russell throughout, and the Celtics were never really in the game at all.

The Warriors' confidence was buoyed tremendously by the way they had manhandled the Celtics. Yet they never won another game that season.

The fourth game was also played at the Cow Palace. It attracted a record turn-away crowd, and their cries urged on the Warriors throughout the evening.

The teams battled almost evenly for two quarters, though the San Franciscans were able to overcome the aggressive Celtic defenses, the continual hacking, jabbing and grabbing, to build a 52–49 lead at the halfway mark.

Through the first half Wilt and Russell played one another magnificently. Wilt won a wide rebound advantage, but Russell kept Chamberlain's point production to a mere 11. In essence, what was happening was that their titanic man-to-man struggle was serving to nullify the effectiveness of each.

It was Tom Heinsohn who broke the game open. Wearing a white bandage over his eye as a result of a first quarter injury, a feature which added to the almost bizarre nature of the wild spectacle he launched, Heinsohn began his spurt when the Celtics were trailing 52–49. He hit for a three-pointer, then a tip-in and then a jumper.

K. C. Jones scored with a pair of foul shots. Then Heinsohn went on his frenzied way again. He added a pair of hook shots, a lay-up and another jumper. Boston's lead was 14 points and the game was on ice for the Celtics.

The Warriors did try to come back. Guy Rodgers spearheaded a late drive that pulled the San Franciscans within one point of the Celts, 92–91. The crowd pleaded, but the Warriors could not muster the final push. Havlicek scored and then Russell. The final score was 98–95.

Two days later in Boston the Warriors fought valiantly to stave off the defeat that most observers now said was inevitable. The team was seriously hobbled by injuries. Rodgers had a dislocated thumb, Meschery twisted an ankle and was benched, Wilt tore a gouge in the palm of his right hand in a fall he had taken and the injury bled throughout the game. Of course, his ball handling was hampered.

The game was a rugged one, the teams pressing one another every step of the way. The lead changed hands a dozen times in the early stages.

With a minute to go in the game, the Celtics clung to a five point advantage, 100–95. Then Attles hit a lay-up off a fast break, and the margin was cut to three points. Sam Jones netted a foul for Boston, and then Wilt, with 19 seconds left, fired a one-hander that brought the San Franciscans within a single field goal of the enemy.

They never got any closer. With 10 seconds remaining, Tommy Heinsohn let go an errant hook shot. But Russell was there and his huge hands fastened upon the ball as if it were a grapefruit. Into the basket he crammed it, and that was that.

Wilt, his injured right hand wrapped in a blood-stained towel, walked slump-shouldered from the court. Fans flooded about him and some jeered. He watched as a swirling mass of Boston enthusiasts hoisted Bill Russell to their shoulders and carried him triumphantly from the court. Wilt shook his head. He wondered if he was ever, ever going to get that kind of treatment.

22

Bellyache

WILT HAD NEVER really wanted to go to San Francisco to play for the Warriors. When the franchise switch was announced, Wilt told Eddie Gottlieb that he wasn't going.

"You can't quit!" Gotty protested, and he explained to Wilt that he was an essential part of the package. If Wilt didn't go there was no deal and as Gottlieb knew full well, "once in a lifetime" deals come only, well, once in a lifetime.

Because Gotty wanted him to, Wilt went to San Francisco. "I owe Eddie everything I have," Wilt has said more than once. "He needed me. So I signed."

Now Wilt was very glad he did.

Losing to the Celtics was certainly no disgrace. Everyone was calling them a superteam. They had now won six championships in a row. No team in any sport—not the Yankees in baseball nor the Canadiens in ice hockey—had ever done that before. The dictionary says "super" means "greater or better than others," and that aptly described the Celtics of 1964.

The season of 1963–1964 could easily be rated as Wilt's most satisfying in basketball up to that time. It was more than winning the Western Division championship, and the fact that the U. S. Basketball Writers Association had voted him the league's Most Valuable Player.

The sports fans of San Francisco now held Wilt in the highest esteem. In their estimation he had, indeed, become "the Willie Mays of basketball." Several times during the season Wilt's exploits at the Cow Palace had won him thundering standing ovations from the crowds that thronged into the arena. Never before in his career had Wilt received that kind of adulation.

The criticism that he was not a team player had been muzzled—at least temporarily. Now when he picked up a newspaper and turned to the sports pages often he would see his skills applauded in glowing terms.

Wilt enjoyed a warm relationship with his Warrior teammates. Al Attles and Guy Rodgers were his closest chums, but every member of the team admired him for his will to do everything possible to help the Warriors win.

In one game he had even coached the team—and with immense success. It happened early in the season at Cincinnati. Coach Hannum was banished from the game in the first quarter for disputing a play. As he walked from the arena, he said to Wilt, "You run the team from out here (the court) and Sears will make the substitutions." Wilt did as he was asked. And he engineered a victory for the Warriors. He also ran up 49 of the 98 points the team gathered.

When the final buzzer sounded, Wilt's face was wreathed in a wide smile. "I told them what I thought would work," he said, "and I got their cooperation."

Another reason for Wilt's contentment was the City

of San Francisco itself. Its sophistication appealed to him. It reminded him of some of the larger cities in Europe of which he had become so fond.

Wilt leased a luxurious two bedroom decorator-furnished apartment in the exclusive Pacific Heights section of the city. He became a sail-boating enthusiast and many of his off-the-court hours were spent on the waters of San Francisco Bay.

He still had his interest in automobiles. But now his affluence enabled him to own a $20,000 Bentley, and he enjoyed the auto without the NCAA calling once.

During the summer Wilt tended to his many and assorted business interests. Villa Chamberlain, his apartment house in West Los Angeles, was in operation now and requiring more of his attention than before.

Wilt kept himself in good physical shape. The summer before he had ballooned to a bulging 330 pounds. Getting into playing condition had been accomplished at great labor, and he had no will to go through such a struggle again.

Sometimes during the summer, back in the blazing heat of New York, he would play basketball with a handful of former college basketball stars from the metropolitan area on the blacktopped outdoor court of a Harlem playground. Though just informal games, they would draw crowds of up to a thousand people and the spectators would jam six and seven deep around the tall wire fencing that surrounded the court. An intrepid few would perch precariously atop the screening to watch the action.

Then in the privacy of a gym, Wilt practiced foul shooting during the summer. His average from the free throw line over the previous season had hardly improved from his early days with the Philadelphia Warriors. It was only 53 percent. He was determined to improve during the coming year, so once again he changed his style. From the underhand motion urged upon him by Cy Kaselman, and later Frank McGuire, Wilt switched to a soft overhand push, aiming for the rim.

All seemed serene with Wilt. But days of dark disappointment were just ahead.

The trouble started simply enough—with a bellyache.

Beginning in mid-summer, Wilt came to be plagued by severe and recurrent pains in his stomach and chest. He had no idea what caused them. He only knew his stomach hurt—and bad. At first he thought it might only be his careless eating habits. For example, hot dogs had been a mainstay of his diet for years. Though not noted for their nutritive value nor for the ease with which they can be digested, frankfurters, in the world of the professional basketball player, have the great advantage of always being available.

Nevertheless Wilt banished hot dogs from his diet and tried to exercise greater control of what he ate and when he ate. Still the pains persisted.

In August, when Wilt appeared in the annual benefit game at Kutshers for Maurice Stokes, he appeared to be in fine fettle, not bothered at all by any stomach ailment. He was not even troubled by a new regulation of the NBA's which prescribed a wider foul lane.

Some observers said the new rule was aimed directly at Wilt. The widening of the lane meant the "safe" area close to the basket was reduced considerably. Alex Hannum was one of the first to cry out against the regulation, and he charged it was discriminatory against Wilt and the Warriors.

But in the Stokes game, Wilt gave not the slightest hint the rule was going to bother him, and he was voted the game's Most Valuable Player. Hannum, who attended the contest, said Wilt looked in great shape and the coach was enthusiastic about the upcoming season.

In the weeks that followed the game at Kutshers, Wilt's stomach brought him more suffering. The pain was really intense now. Often his stomach and lower chest felt as if they were filled with hot coals.

In mid-September, when he arrived in San Francisco for the opening of the Warrior training season, his illness was a cause of deep worry to him. It was not only the repeated pain that troubled him; not knowing what caused it was just as bad.

A few days after his arrival in San Francisco, the Warriors were scheduled to meet the United States Olympic Team then in training for the Tokyo Games, with the proceeds of the contest to go to the U. S. Olympic Fund.

Hannum was determined to win the game, even though it was only an exhibition, but both he and the Warriors underestimated their foes. (The team went on to win the Olympic championship.) Compared to the well-conditioned Olympians, the Warriors looked slow and sluggish. The San Franciscans fell behind early and were never able to make up the gap.

After the game, Wilt's stomach miseries broke out anew. He confessed his condition to Hannum and to the team physician, Dr. Dudley Fournier. A hospital checkup was advised and Wilt took the advice.

"Wilt really must be hurting," said Warrior owner Frank Mieuli (he had assumed Eddie Gottlieb's stock holdings in the team). "He never complains after a game about being banged around, and he gets banged around plenty."

So as the Warrior team left San Francisco on its exhibition schedule through the Pacific Northwest, Wilt lay in St. Mary's hospital in San Francisco, the first time in his career that he had been sidelined. This fact weighed upon him as much as his pain and his illness, whatever that illness might be.

Now began a long series of poking and probing

Wilt's massive frame. It was often a painful siege, always an uncomfortable one.

The first bulletin issued by the corps of doctors ministering to him declared that Wilt was a victim of "gastroenteritis," a medical term that meant the patient's stomach lining and intestines were inflamed and sore. That was scarcely news to Wilt.

Wilt's hospital stay stretched to a week, then two weeks and then more. September melted into October, and the opening of the league season loomed large on the calendar, and still the doctors continued to explore Wilt's body for the cause of the pain. He was becoming more and more disgusted now, and his morale was not improved any by reports that came to him about the Warriors.

They were floundering disasterously through the exhibition schedule, losing many more games than they were winning.

Dick Freindlich of the San Francisco *Chronicle* visited Wilt in the hospital and Wilt told him he was being treated by three doctors, Dr. Good News, Dr. Bad News, and Dr. No News.

"Dr. Good News comes in," Wilt said, "and he says, 'Don't worry, Wilt, you'll be skiing next week.'

"Then Dr. Bad News comes in, and he says, 'Wilt, you might as well make up your mind, you're going to be here for a while.'

"Then Dr. No News comes in. He just shakes his head and says nothing."

One of the reports that leaked from the hospital stated Wilt was being treated for a heart ailment. Tests showed, said this report, that there was an irregularity to the manner in which Chamberlain's heart functioned. Indeed, there was, but this was not new information to Wilt. The abnormality had been uncovered by doctors long before, but its nature was such that it had no effect upon Wilt's general well being.

The daily newspapers played up the news, a fact that further upset Wilt. He was worried what his parents would think. "The only heart attack there's going to be will be the one my mother has when she reads that story."

Meanwhile Hannum's dreams of a brilliant season for the Warriors were beginning to explode. More and more he became resigned to the fact that the team would be starting the season without the big man.

Nate Thurmond was being groomed as a cornerman, but with Wilt out, Nate was moved back to the pivot position. "It's going to take time for him to readjust," Hannum said. "He spent the whole summer learning to shoot from the outside."

At the forward positions, Hannum now planned to use Wayne Hightower and Tom Meschery, but the latter had broken his hand during the summer and though it was on the mend, Meschery was far from being in peak form.

The Warrior predicament was clear. With Wilt out, scoring production was going to be reduced by about 40 points a game. No team can be struck that type of a blow and expect to be successful, no matter what type of player juggling is done. Hannum knew this and his moans could be heard coast-to-coast.

Shortly before the season opened, Wilt was released from the hospital, but he knew little more about his condition at the time of his release than he knew when he first entered. What the doctors had done was establish a number of "non-causes" for Wilt's pains. For example, they knew the pain was *not* caused by an ulcer. "What *was* causing the pain?" Wilt protested. Nobody knew for sure.

Wilt's remorse was now greater than ever. He was still sick; he still didn't know why.

In the three weeks he had spent in the hospital bed he lost 35 pounds and had grown considerably

weaker. He was in poorer condition now than he had
been on the day the training season had opened.

But he was still determined to find the cause of his
pain, which now had such a mysterious quality about it,
so he decided he would return to Philadelphia and see
his own physician, Dr. Stanley Lorber of Temple University Hospital. And as he prepared to board the
plane that would take him east, the Warriors opened
up the season in defense of their Western Division
title.

At Temple University Hospital—at last—the cause
of Wilt's pain and sickness was determined. The problem said the doctors was with his pancreas, a finger-
sized gland located behind the stomach, that produces
juices that aid in the digestive process. Wilt's discom-
fort was being caused because of an inflamed pancreas,
and this, in turn, was brought on by a malfunction of a
thyroid gland. The doctors had a name for Wilt's
affliction: they called it "pancreatitis."

"Can it be cured?" was Wilt's first question. Probably not completely, at least not right away, the doctors
said. But by medication and proper control of his diet
Wilt could improve his condition.

Next, of course, Wilt wanted to know if he could
play basketball over the season ahead. The doctors
said they didn't think he should. "Take a layoff," they
told him. "Rest for two or three months." Then the
plan was to re-examine Wilt again to see if the rest had
worked any improvement. If it had, he would be allowed to play ball.

But Wilt could not bring himself to follow that advice. He felt the team depended on him. He could not
let them down. He would play.

His two year contract was to expire at the end of the
season. When it did, he decided he would call it quits.

23

Grim Season

THE FANS WHO had wondered how San Francisco would fare without Wilt in the line-up quickly found out—to their immense distress.

The Warriors had come to depend on Wilt more than anyone realized. They relied on his ability to score. They depended on him in the pivot to work their cut-offs. With him they had carved out a division championship. Now, just a few months later, they were sick without him. Of the first eight games they played, they won only one and that was close.

Nate Thurmond did a fine job of filling in for Wilt. Though he lacked Chamberlain's experience, and showed it in his inability to pace himself, he performed tremendously as a rebounder and impressed observers with his fine assortment of hook shots and jumpers. "He's young and he has great potential," said Hannum of Thurmond. "I wouldn't trade him for any center in the league right now."

When Wilt did return to the Warrior line-up he was well below his playing weight and out of condition from lying in hospital beds. "He's a very tired man," Hannum said of him. His timing was off, and he was unable to hit his shots with anywhere near his usual consistency.

Slowly Wilt played himself back into shape. It took time and it wasn't until mid-November that he approached his usual form. By that time, the Warriors had sunk into last place. Team morale was at a low ebb.

In fairness to the other players, it must be said that a number of them were hindered by nagging injuries. Rodgers, Meschery, Attles and Gary Phillips were all sidelined at one time or another during the early stages of the season.

As loss piled upon loss, the players' disgust grew. Their low spirits were reflected in their play. Nobody was moving and Wilt was being forced to shoot whether he wanted to or not. The headlines began to have a familiar look. "Wilt Nets 53; Warriors Lose" or "Chamberlain Scores 62 in Losing Effort." Deeper and deeper into the cellar the team plunged.

It all reminded Wilt of his sophomore year in the league when he was playing with Philadelphia. And just as in that season, now he was having the same old trouble from the free throw line. For foul shooting, his average for the season tumbled to below .600.

The soft push shot that he had been using had failed him, so Hannum got him to change to a hard bank. That proved even worse. So he switched back to the feathery push, and later in the season, when his average dipped below .500, he reverted to the underhand style again.

When a team, not a team of has-beens or never-will-bes, but a team of solid skills—as the Warriors were—begins to lose consistently, the players seethe. They grow tense; they press to win. And their anxiety breeds still more failure. So it was with the San Franciscans and Wilt.

As the team continued to lose, tension built upon tension, and Chamberlain bore the brunt of the strain. Each game the furrows in his brow grew deeper and his elbows flashed with greater fury than ever in close-up play.

In a game in New York, he scuffled with Bob Boozer of the Knickerbockers, a former Kansas teammate of Wilt's and a good chum. After the game, Boozer shrugged it off. "Poor Wilt," he said. "He used to be a happy guy and easy-going. He's tense and irritable and real aggravated."

Now rumors began to float about that Chamberlain was going to be traded. Daily newspapers in every part of the country headlined the talk, and reporters everywhere asked Wilt what was what. Wilt had to admit he was in complete ignorance about the reports. And, in truth, none of the officials of the San Francisco team had said a word to Wilt about the trade talk and whether it was true or not.

Then things got even worse.

It happened during a game at the Civic Auditorium in San Francisco. The Warriors were hosts to the Boston Celtics. Amazingly the San Franciscans got away to a quick and substantial lead. By late in the second quarter they had stretched their advantage over the Bostonians to a marvelous 30 points, and Red Auerbach conceded defeat by resting his regulars.

One of the replacement troops the Boston coach thrust into the Celtic line-up was a bruising 6 feet 10 inch, 230 pound rookie named John Thompson. Minutes after he strode out on to the court, Thompson made what up to that time was the most distinctive move of his career. In a struggle for the ball under the San Francisco basket, Thompson unleased an elbow and it caught Chamberlain square in the middle of his face; it splattered his nose and broke it.

Again Wilt was out of action, and any hopes the team had of rising in the league standings now seemed doomed. When, a week later, Wilt returned to the line-up, his nose was shielded by a plastic face mask. Combined with a goatee he had cultivated, it made him look like the feature player in a Hollywood horror movie. More important, for a time it served to diminish his accuracy with the ball.

In the brief space of six months a series of events had plummeted the proud Warriors from their status as champions to a role as division tail enders. The fans reacted, as fans do almost everywhere, by staying home. In some games attendance didn't even hit the one thousand mark. Just before the All Star game hiatus, the Warriors went three weeks without a win. Though the calendar said only January, the team was beginning to act like the season was over.

Wilt's morale, in accompaniment to the team's show-ing, was at a desperate low. Sometimes he hoped he would be traded. Sometimes he hoped he wouldn't. Sometimes he thought about quitting. Sometimes he didn't know what to think.

24

Traded

"Trade Wilt Chamberlain?" a fan asked. "How could they possibly do that?"

There were rumors all about Wilt being offered for sale or trade. At first glance they seemed absurd. Here was the greatest all around performer in the history of basketball, a man who had devastated the record books. Now he was at the peak of his career. How could San Francisco allow another team to get its hands on him?

At second glance, however, the idea didn't seem preposterous at all. In fact, there were three very good reasons why the trade made sense.

Number one, the Warriors had *two* excellent centers; Chamberlain and Thurmond, and Thurmond was riding the bench whenever Chamberlain was playing.

Number two was the fact of the Warrior attendance, or lack of attendance. The fans were staying away as they never had before. On the road, Wilt's presence filled many a seat, but under the NBA rules the visiting club takes no share of the road receipts. So Wilt's value as a road attraction was of no benefit to the San Francisco owners.

Reason number three was Wilt's salary, then estimated to be $65,000 a year (whereas Thurmond's was only a fifth of that). Wilt was taking home one dollar out of every three the Warriors took in at the box-office. A situation like that spells calamity for a team.

So late in 1964, the San Francisco Warriors put Wilton Norman Chamberlain on the market.

There may have been an exception or two, but it can be safely said that every team in the NBA wanted Wilt. Not many, however, felt they could afford him, and only three clubs got into serious discussions with the Warrior management for Wilt's services.

The St. Louis Hawks offered money; reports said as much as $200,000, plus a player. The Los Angeles Lakers offered less cash and more players. The Philadelphia 76ers offered mainly players. The Knicks, too, were dealing with the Warriors, but claimed they were more interested in obtaining Thurmond than Chamberlain.

From the start Philadelphia had the edge in the dealings for the simple reason that the 76ers were members of the Eastern Division. Frank Mieuli had no great desire to see Wilt play for Los Angeles or St. Louis, teams that would be trying to outdo the Warriors in the league standings.

At the league All Star game in St. Louis in mid-January, with all the owners in assemblage, the dealings reached their peak, and rumors and bits of fact concerning Chamberlain's future were all but shouted from the roof tops. The talk and the press attention concerning the prospective trade rendered the annual meeting of East vs. West to largely a sideshow status.

The transaction was finalized at close to 1:00 A.M.

at Stan Musial's restaurant where a cheery post-All Star game party was in session. It was planned to delay the official announcement of the trade until an organized press conference could be held, but word of the negotiations leaked out and spread quickly, so a hasty announcement was made then and there.

Philadelphia was the team that had won him. Wilt would be going home.

The dealings between Philadelphia and San Francisco were casual. Late in December, when the Warriors were in Philadelphia to meet the 76ers, Richman made a formal offer for Wilt, with a stipulation that Mieuli give a "yes" or "no" to the offer by January 13, the day of the All Star game. "We felt we couldn't wait any longer than that," Richman said. "We needed someone, and if we didn't land Wilt we needed time to try some place else."

When Richman arrived in St. Louis he met with Mieuli and repeated the offer. Mieuli listened and shrugged. "We thought the deal was dead," Richman said. "We were getting ready to leave the party when Mieuli walked up at two minutes before 12 o'clock and said, 'You got a deal.' "

Whether the 76ers gave up any cash to obtain Wilt has never been revealed. The official announcement said "an undisclosed sum" was involved. If, indeed, any money did change hands, it was not a great amount —less than $50,000.

Philadelphia did agree to send three players to the Warriors, Lee Shaffer, a holdout, Connie Dierking, an injury case, and Paul Neuman, a three-year man with the league and probably the best player of the lot. If anything, the three were distinguished by a lack of distinction.

Of course, Philadelphia would also be assuming Wilt's salary, and that, to the San Francisco owners, was the most important factor in the whole business.

To Wilt the trade was an extreme disappointment. He did not mind being traded. He realized that player trades are as much a part of professional basketball as midnight airplane rides.

But the reason for Wilt's disappointment had to do with one Ike Richman, principal owner of the 76ers. Richman, a Philadelphia lawyer, and Chamberlain were longtime friends. Often Richman counseled Wilt in financial and legal matters.

Wilt had asked Ike not to deal for him, disclosing that he planned to quit at the end of the season. As Wilt saw it, in three months he would be out of basketball and Richman would be out three players and whatever cash he had put up.

"When I retire after this season, people will say I walked out on a friend," Wilt lamented to Milt Gross of the New York *Post*, after the trade.

Richman, however, wasn't worried about future seasons. "I think we can talk him into playing for us," he said. What did concern him was the present.

His 76ers had won about half of their games, and they rested securely in second place. In Hal Greer and Larry Costello they had the fastest pair of guards in the NBA, and both were renowned for their ability as outside shooters. But the team was weak in the pivot where Johnny Kerr, 32, and a 10-year veteran with the league, was faltering. Rebounding was another of the 76ers' deficiencies, though a husky rookie named Lucius Jackson had been an unexpected help in that department.

The thought of working with Greer and Costello brightened the picture considerably for Wilt. "Maybe for the first time they'll have to play me honestly," he said. "It's got to be better for me on this team."

Richman granted Wilt a week's leave of absence before joining his new mates, time he needed to settle personal and business affairs in San Francisco. When

Wilt's plane arrived in Philadelphia and he clambered down the ramp into a waiting throng of reporters, photographers and television cameramen, a broad grin was on his face. It was good to be back.

Not a soul was prepared for the reception that the Philadelphians were to give to Wilt. Certainly Richman, who was in a better position to know than anyone, had no anticipation of what was going to happen. He admitted he didn't expect Wilt was going to bring in people unless the team developed into a winning one. After all, an important factor in the Warrior's departure to San Francisco two and one-half years before had been the general air of indifference the fans had displayed toward Wilt. But, my, how the situation had changed.

Anyone who witnessed Wilt's Great Return will never forget it. Even experienced newspapermen, veterans of championship football games and innumerable World Series games, recall the night as one of the most thrilling in sports.

The 76ers faced Wilt's ex-teammates, the Warriors, who were in the throes of a 13-game losing streak. The 76ers were ousted from Convention Hall by a bowling tournament that was in progress and the game was put into the Arena, a ramshackle undersized battlefield in West Philadelphia, though by pre-Chamberlain standards it was plenty big enough. Richman would have been happy if a crowd of 4,000 had decided to turn out for the game, for 4,000 was well above the 76ers season average. What happened made Ike ecstatic.

There was an excitement on the night of the game, as there is before heavyweight championship matches. You could really feel it. The crowds started early, and an hour before game time traffic was jammed on Market Street outside the Arena. The fans stormed the gates and 6,140 jammed their way in before police ordered the entrances closed. You could not have gotten another person in with a shoehorn. It was the largest crowd anyone could ever remember being packed into the place.

Thousands outside were still trying to fight their way in when Wilt was being introduced to the crowd. He really didn't know what would happen. It wasn't very long ago that the fans' disinterest had driven Wilt and his teammates out of town. And there was talk that the Philadelphians were upset by Wilt's statements that he planned to retire.

"And now," blared the public address system, "Philadelphia's own Wilt Chamberlain." Slowly, his hands clasped behind his back, Wilt walked into the glare of the spotlight. Then came a tremendous roar. The people that weren't already standing got to their feet and gave Wilt a thundering ovation that lasted well over 30 seconds. Said Wilt later: "There never has been anything like that before."

The tingling excitement continued throughout the night. Some people carried signs that proclaimed, "Big Wilt Is Back!" or "Another Dipper Dunk!" It was obvious from the beginning they had come to see Wilt, and only Wilt. When he rebounded, the crowd screamed. When he scored, they roared their approval. And when he dunked the ball, the great shouts of joy could be heard all the way to Camden. It was a hysterical night.

Oh, yes, the 76ers won, and the way they won was significant. Wilt's presence jammed up the inside and made it possible for Greer and Costello to hit from the outside. Greer had 28 points; Costello, 24.

Wilt surprised his new coach Dolf Schayes, never really a Chamberlain booster before, with the way he fired the ball out to trigger the team's fast break. And the protection he gave his teammates on defense was another wonder. Obviously, now the 76ers were a solid challenger to the Celtics.

"It wasn't an overpowering win," said Schayes after the game. "But what impressed me was the way Wilt pitched out in a hurry, and how he sacrificed himself for the team."

Ike Richman was far less restrained. "The big man was fabulous," he said. "He was sensational. I say, look out; we're coming."

Following the high excitement at the Arena, the 76ers departed on a brief road trip through the East. The high point of the swing was in Syracuse where the Philadelphians came face-to-face with the Boston Celtics who were blazing along on a 16-game winning streak. Another Boston victory would enable them to tie the all-time NBA record of 17 victories in a row.

Before a raucous standing-room-only crowd, the rejuvenated 76ers stopped the Celts cold. Wilt, in his personal vendetta with Bill Russell, showed magnificently. Russell took 15 shots and Wilt's harassing hands prevented him from getting a single field goal.

When the 76ers arrived home late in the month to face the Celtics at Convention Hall, they were greeted as if they had just won the NBA championship. There was more excitement than a Mummers Parade, and Philadelphians—10,831 of them—packed Convention Hall to the rafters. The throng smashed all previous attendance records.

What the swarm of fans saw, they loved. Wilt outdid Russell every step of the way. He was his better in scoring, in rebounds, and even in assists and free throws. The Celtics fell to their fourth defeat at the hands of the 76ers, while no other team in the league had been able to beat the Bostonians more than once. For the long suffering Philadelphia fan, it was all too good to be true.

In Wilt's first 11 games with the 76ers, the team won nine, and for a time they mildly threatened the status of the second place St. Louis Hawks. But then

Larry Costello was injured, and forced to ride the bench, and Hal Greer was hurt. With both Costello and Greer out of action, Philadelphia's hopes for a second place finish melted away.

Schayes was in no hurry to put his injured men back into the line-up. He wanted them fully rested and in peak physical form for the playoffs, and there was little sense in having them risk further injury in all but meaningless end-of-the-season games. But this policy put a severe strain on Wilt, who, for most of the tail end of the season, was the team's sole offense and defense.

Just for the record, it should be mentioned that Wilt's former teammates in San Francisco finished the season about as deep in last place as they could possibly get. They achieved the wretched distinction of becoming the losingest team in the history of the NBA. No less than 63 times were they floored for the count. To Wilt the trade that sent him to Philadelphia was looking better all the time.

25

Home Sweet Home

THE OUTCOME of every professional basketball game, as anyone the least bit familiar with the sport realizes, is deeply affected by what is known as the home court advantage—the benefits that accrue to a team which plays in familiar surroundings and before friendly fans.

Make no mistake, the home court advantage is no myth. Indeed, in the National Basketball Association, the home team wins as much as 70 percent of the time —in Boston's case, it is more than 80 percent—and Las Vegas oddsmakers judge playing at home to be worth five to eight points to a team. Dolf Schayes has said the Boston Garden is worth at least 10 points a game to the Celtics.

Why? Why should skilled players, seasoned through four years of college basketball and additional years of professional experience, competing in modern arenas and on courts all precisely the same size (except Madison Square Garden where the floor is six inches shorter in length than the standard 94 feet by 50 feet), be so significantly influenced by the home advantage?

There are many reasons. First of all, on their home court players become familiar with the way the court is lighted and with the resiliency of the backboard.

Some other reasons are psychological. There are the fans, for instance. Says one player: "When you've got ten thousand or so fans screaming and booing at you and you're trying to get set to shoot a foul shot, it's easy to get the iron suit (*choke-up*)."

The treatment the visitors get from the hometown management may not always be noted for its good fellowhood. The heat in the dressing room may leave something to be desired; hot showers often don't exist. "Philadelphia is a bush town," Red Auerbach once snarled, "You ask for 11 orange juices and you're sure to get 10." Such abuses register with the players.

Then there are the referees. Most coaches feel that the refs, at least subconciously, are affected by the raucous screams of the hometown supporters. Players *know* they are.

Few times in the history of the National Basketball Association playoffs has the home court advantage been so pronounced as it was in 1965. Except for a momentary lapse or two, Wilt played the most splendid basketball of his career during these playoffs, but he and the 76ers ran into the concept of home court advantage just as surely as if it were a 12-foot brick wall. The Celtics did, too. But unfortunately, the series opened in Boston and—inevitably—closed there.

Before taking on Boston, the 76ers first disposed of the Cincinnati Royals in the semi-final playoff series, and they did it without great hardship.

About two weeks before the semi-finals opened, Wilt's pancreas burst into pain, the same burning pain he had experienced before. At one stage it became so agonizing he had to bench himself in the final moments of a late season game. But doctors were able to quell the pain enough to allow Wilt to take part in the playoffs.

By this time Wilt's pancreas was as famous around the league as Jimmy Durante's schnozzola is in the show-business world, and it was being subjected to much the same good-natured ridicule.

Said Cincinnati coach Jack McMahon before the playoff series: "We might try hitting Wilt in the pancreas, but how am I going to tell anyone where the pancreas is?" But to Wilt the matter was never laughable, and he made plans to enter the famed Mayo Clinic in Rochester, Minnesota, when the season was over to see if his painful condition might be corrected.

The Royals were not up to par either, for Oscar Robertson was hindered by a strained tendon in his left foot, and with the Big O's maneuverability trimmed, Cincinnati's chances to beat the Philadelphians shrank dramatically.

The first game of the three-out-of-five set was the most important. Though it was played at Cincinnati, the 76ers won it. A 20-foot jump shot by Al Bianchi tied the game at the final buzzer, and a pair of free throws by Wilt provided the margin of victory in the overtime session.

In the second game, the phenomenal Robertson, despite his aching back, broke loose to score 40 points and the Royals won. They won no more after that. With Wilt and a hustling Al Bianchi leading the way, the 76ers closed the door, but it was Wilt who was the dominating force. He led the team in scoring, he blocked shots and rebounded with a vengeance, and even sagged off to help his Philadelphia mates thwart Robertson.

The 76ers locker room was noisily good-natured after the wind-up game against the Royals, and there were shouts of, "Bring on the Celtics." But Wilt was a bit grim. Too often he had gone in against the Bostonians brimming over with confidence, only to have that confidence quickly shattered.

There was a saying around the league now that declared, "The Celtics always win the seventh game." The record book attested to the veracity of the statement. The Bostonians had won an unprecedented six National Championships in succession. They also could claim nine consecutive Eastern Division Championships. Wilt had belief in his ability and in the team's, but he also bore a great and quiet respect for the Celtics, and for Russell, Heinsohn, Sanders, K. C. Jones, Havlicek and for Sam Jones, now rated as the top scorer in Celtic history with a 25.9 game average over the season.

In the very first game of the division finals, with the Boston Garden packed to capacity (13,909 is the figure the management always announces), the Celtics launched an all court press, a device for which they had won wide fame. It worked—quickly and with extraordinary success. Before the buzzer sounded to signal the end of the first quarter, the game's outcome had been decided.

The purpose of a full court pressing defense is to impede the offensive team from moving the ball into the front court. The harassment delays the ball's advance by eight to ten seconds. Then another ten seconds is involved in getting the play set, in cutting and screening. The net result is that the team in possession often has to hurry its shot to keep within the 24-second limit.

The press is not an out-an-out attempt to gain possession of the ball. But in the fury of the press, passes are deflected and loose balls occur.

A parenthetical thought should be interjected here. Today, in professional basketball, where players shoot with fierce accuracy, a team that loses possession of the ball often commits a four point error—the two points that are lost for not scoring, and the two points the opposition does score. A stolen ball or a pass that goes astray is a grievous matter.

The pressing defense works with most devastating effect on one's home court. This is partly because the hometown fans, by their shouts and screams, add to the strain and stress put on the opposition.

The fans also serve to aid the referees. Shouts like, "Watch, Greer, he's walking!" do indeed put a referee on the alert.

In their first game at Boston, the 76ers showed with crystal clarity how demoralizing the full court press can be. A dozen times they lost the ball in the backcourt during the first half, and ten minutes of the first period went by before they could work the ball in to Wilt for a shot. All the while the Boston fans were urging on their defenders, and all the while Heinsohn, Naulls and Sanders were hitting—and with their usual consistency —from the corners. Facts like these spell out disaster.

Wilt was superb, and Schayes was to declare, "He's playing the best ball of his career."

From the opening tip, Chamberlain completely overpowered and overshadowed Russell. He out-rebounded the league's Most Valuable Player, too, and with 33 points, out-scored him on a three-to-one ratio, and this despite Russell himself who was positioned behind him, and K. C. Jones and Sanders who sagged off in front.

Two days later the teams clashed again, this time at Convention Hall. Said Auerbach: "The people down there sit right next to the court. They're on the players and referees all the time." He called the 76ers' home grounds a "snakepit."

In the three games that were to be played at Convention Hall, the Celtics never failed to apply the full court press, but they were also never able to achieve the success with it they enjoyed at Boston. The 76ers upset the device mostly by the use of long, clothesline passes to the cornermen or to Wilt. Often these men would come back to screen or meet the pass.

Again Wilt played with sheer brilliance. He racked up 30 points, to 12 for Russell, and he outdazzled the *other* bearded pillar in rebounding by an astonishing 39–16 count. "Every game against Wilt is three days' work," said Russell.

The series stood tied at 1–1, and now it was back to Boston again.

Again the press, and again the Celtics used it with the same startling efficiency they had in the first game; in fact, the whole play of the game was a carbon copy of what had happened at the Garden just a few days before. The 76ers were completely disorganized by Boston's spirited defense, and they were unable to get the ball out of the backcourt with any degree of competence.

During the first half Wilt, if he had brought along a deck of cards, could have played a game of solitaire, for he rarely had an opportunity to make an offensive move. The same could be said for the 76ers' cornermen. Statistics tell the story: in the first half, Philadelphia's forwards and the pivot—Wilt—accounted for only five baskets. That's how effective the Celtics' press was.

Sam Jones and Havlicek were popping one-handers from the outside and Russell was hitting, too, on soft tap-ins and lay-ups as Wilt faltered on defense.

Some walking violations and some three-second infractions were called against Wilt, and once he fired a pass to Lucius Jackson who was standing out-of-bounds. It was Chamberlain's poorest game of the seven.

Wilt made no newspaper headlines with his on-the-court performance in game three, but he certainly did with a magazine article he had prepared some weeks before and the publisher now decided to release. *Sports Illustrated* was the name of the publication. "My Life in the Bush League" was the title of the article. It was, in many ways, a startlingly frank and often revealing player's-eye-view of the pressures of professional basketball.

The article was jam-packed with criticism, and spoke disapprovingly of NBA basketball, in general, league officials, owners, particularly Frank Mieuli of San Francisco, and coaches, with Wilt's own coach, Dolf Schayes, coming in for some pretty stiff ridicule. Wilt characterized Schayes as being too "gentle and soft-hearted" and "too nice a guy to coach a bunch of hardened basketball professionals."

The piece stirred up a hornets' nest. Everyone had a comment to make pro or con, but mostly con. The consensus of his teammates was that Wilt was out of place in criticizing his coach.

For his part, Wilt protested the magazine had distorted what he had said in his interview, and that the publication had introduced many "unauthorized thoughts" into the text without his consent. Wilt declared the article had caused him embarrassment and humiliation and he said he contemplated legal action against the magazine.

The timing of the article, coming as it did in the midst of the playoffs, was particularly unfortunate. However, most of the 76ers felt it wouldn't hurt the team. Of course it didn't help, and it had the tangible effect of serving to make relations between Wilt and Dolf Schayes quite frosty.

Gordon Forbes of the Philadelphia *Inquirer* summed up the situation best when he commented, "It appears Wilt has stuffed one in the wrong basket."

For the fourth game the action returned to Philadelphia, where the home court advantage worked again, though it took an over-time period before the magic prevailed.

Regulation play ended on an incredible note. In the last second of play, Hall Greer grabbed a pass, and from 30 feet away, jumped, spun and threw all in one fluid motion. The ball swished through the net as the final buzzer sounded.

Throughout the game, Wilt was again in peak form. Again he out-shone Russell, going over him for 34 points.

In the fifth game at Boston, where the Celtics' "Green Wave" surged down the court time and time again before the 76ers' defenders could set themselves, and in the sixth game in Philadelphia, where Wilt's pressure tip near the end to Greer, who banged in a 25-footer, was the highlight, the home court advantage proved the telling factor.

So, as it always seems to, the series came down to the seventh game.

In playoff contests and in regular season games over the two previous years, the 76ers had managed to lose 11 consecutive games at Boston Garden. Schayes now was more determined than ever to upset the jinx, and he looked for Wilt to be the key factor. Said Schayes: "Wilt has gone through six years of frustration trying to win this championship. I'm sure he'll come up with that one game that will help us do it."

Schayes was asked why the 76ers always seemed so inadequate in Boston. "Pressure! Pressure!" he replied. "Some of our younger players still haven't gotten over the fear of the Boston floor. They see how tough it is for us up there, and in their minds it becomes even tougher."

In all too typical fashion, the Celtics raced to a quick lead, and before the first period was over, the Bostonians led by 18 points. But Wilt, Chet Walker and Dave Gambee, who was filling in for Larry Costello, launched a glorious effort and propelled the 76ers in a 62–61 halftime lead.

Throughout the third period and into the fourth, the game seesawed back and forth.

With four and one-half minutes remaining, the Celtics were on top, 104–103. Then the Boston team delivered what they hoped was the crusher. Sam Jones scored on a jump behind a screen. Havlicek and Russell pushed in free throws. Then Sanders stole a pass and quickly the Boston lead spiraled to 110–103.

There were less than two minutes to play now. If the 76ers were to win or to tie they would need a miracle. Somehow Wilt brought the team back, and he did it singlehandedly in what was one of his greatest court performances.

Wilt's quick tip-in made it 110–105. Then he was fouled, and he lofted in both free throws. It was Boston's ball, they gave it to Sam Jones and he dribbled out the clock. A few seconds later Wilt crammed in a stuffer, Russell cringing to avoid causing a foul. Now the score stood at 110–109, and the shrieks of the fans were enough to split Wilt's head.

But the tragedy of it was that only six seconds remained now, and it was Boston's ball. Bill Russell was the man elected to throw it in. He pushed a high pass but it never made its intended receiver. Instead it struck the rim of the Boston basket and caromed out of bounds. Philadelphia took possession. An incredible break.

Immediately Schayes called a time out. There were just five seconds on the clock when his players gathered about him. Schayes set the strategy. The play was to be this: Greer was to throw an in-bounds pass to Walker. While Johnny Kerr built a screen, Walker was to fire back to Greer, and then the team's best outside shooter would take the final shot. Wilt was to station himself under the basket, alert to guide the shot in.

It was a solid play. "I would have called the exact same thing," Wilt was to say later. But Greer never got to make his shot. Hal arced the pass to Walker, but never saw Boston's Johnny Havlicek who managed to get an arm high over Walker's head, and as the ball came toward the pair, Havlicek batted it across the mid-court line. Sam Jones stooped to grab it as the final buzzer sounded.

The errant pass washed out the 76ers' stirring comeback. And Chamberlain's magnificence in the final minutes and, in fact, through the entire series, was wholly buried by the conclusiveness of defeat.

Three times now in his six year career Wilt had managed to make the division finals. One other time he had fought it out for the league championship. And in every case the Celtics had turned him back, but now the defeat seemed more bitter than ever before, for the "non-champion" tag seemed more irrefutable than ever.*

The fans, even in enemy Boston, had come to a realization of Wilt's frustration. As he made his way from the court, they gathered about him and one clapped him on the back and said, "You were great, Wilt." And another echoed, "Simply great." He acknowledged their kindness with a brief nod, but he could not manage a smile.

And over in the Boston dressing room, Bill Russell, surrounded by reporters, spoke of Wilt's sterling play throughout the series, and noting that he had been turned back again in his quest for a championship, Russell declared, "I think in the not too distant future he'll get it."

* See publisher's note, page 184.

26

"You're Too Tall, Wilt!"

MOST OBSERVERS AGREE that the 1965–1966 season was Wilt's finest in basketball. And for a time it was his most gratifying. For only a brief time, however.

Not many weeks before the season opened, Wilt ended months of speculation about his future when he signed a three-year contract with the 76ers, calling for an annual salary in six figures. "We believe it to be the largest contract in organized sports," said 76er owner Irv Kosloff in announcing Wilt's signing. That would put Wilt in the $125,000-a-year class.

During the early stages of the season, the 76ers were slotted third, but after the All Star hiatus they began to surge. They passed Cincinnati and then, by virtue of a glittering 11 game winning streak in the last two weeks of the season, they charged to the league championship, finishing one game ahead of the Celtics. They thereby ended Boston's nine year reign as division champions.

In every quarter Wilt was hailed as the key in the 76ers' great triumph. Again he was the league's scoring leader. (Late in the season he broke Bob Pettit's career scoring record of 20,880 points.) He also took down the rebound title which he had relinquished to Bill Russell the previous two seasons. But it was Wilt's fine team play that won the loudest applause.

"Wilt's tougher to play now than he's ever been," said Knicks' center Walt Bellamy. "You never know what he's going to do. Before, you knew he would go for the basket. Now, you've got to think who he's going to pass to."

There were accolades of more tangible nature. Dolf Schayes was named NBA Coach of the Year and Wilt won election as the league's Most Valuable Player.

There was great joy and jubilation, and it lasted for 18 days.

In the semi-final playoffs, it took only five games for the Celtics to whip the 76ers and whisk the Eastern Division championship back to Boston.

The Philadelphians were flat and often disorganized. The one game they did win they came close to blowing.

Only Luke Jackson gave Wilt any consistent help in rebounding. The team's shooting was atrocious and more than once the 76ers lost their poise.

In the final game, Wilt put forth a desperate last ditch effort to stave off defeat. He scored 46 points and pulled down 34 rebounds, but no one helped, and defeat, which had loomed almost inevitable from the first game, settled upon them.

Critics again pointed accusingly at Wilt.

Wilt's failure to appear at pre-playoff practice sessions caused reams of comment. This was cited as evidence of Schayes' inability to control the team and contributory to the shellacking the Celtics had handed them. In truth, Wilt had a flu infection and a 102-degree temperature to go with it, and he had been excused from the practice sessions.

Bill Russell, in a post playoff interview, did not help matters. He said Boston's success was due to the fact the Celtics played the game as a five-man team sport; he implied the 76ers did not and that was their failing.

Wilt protested the raps. "I played better basketball in the last series than I ever did in my whole life," he told Milt Gross. But no one was listening.

It was as it always has been for Wilt. The same monumental problem beleaguers him. Because he is 7 feet tall, the world expects him to be superhuman.

He is not; but unfailingly he's judged by "super" standards.

Wilt Chamberlain has thoroughly devastated basketball's record books, and while he may not have revolutionized the game, his skills have served to change it more than a little.

Will anyone *ever* surpass Wilt's individual scoring feats? It is not likely.

Will anyone ever attain the commanding status Wilt now holds in the pro game? It is not likely.

Yet in every part of the country fans hoot and jeer at him. Referees, opposing players, coaches and club owners have demeaned his skills. He was a favored target of the NCAA, and through the years basketball's rulemakers have tried to cut his talents down to a less awesome dimension.

The press gives him only erratic support at best. "Wary," "aloof" and "abrupt" are adjectives writers use to describe him.

It was late in the 1966 season when Wilt and his 76er teammates were locked in their fierce struggle with both the Cincinnati Royals and the Boston Celtics for the league lead. Less than two games separated the three teams.

The 76ers came into Madison Square Garden following a defeat at home the night before, and there a spirited Knick team beat them soundly.

Wilt played poorly.

After the game, he showered, dressed and, carrying his equipment bag, left the steamy locker room. He made his way slowly through the dimly lit passageway at the rear of the now silent arena, and emerged through the players' exit onto a side street. The cold wind of the February night slammed into him, and he pulled the collar of his short camel hair topcoat tight about his throat.

Groups of youngsters seeking autographs were clustered on the street outside, and when they spotted Wilt, they converged on him. "Wilt! Wilt! Please sign this." They pressed pencils, program books and scraps of paper on him.

Wilt shook his head slowly. "No," he murmured. A plane was waiting at LaGuardia Field to take the team to Boston for the next day's game. He had to hurry. He turned and, hip deep in youngsters, started down the dark, wind-whipped street.

In the lot at the rear of the Garden was Wilt's car. It was parked close to the one adjacent and he wasn't able to get the door open wide enough to enter. He tried to squeeze his huge frame through but he couldn't.

The youngsters stood and watched and one, seeing his plight, yelled out, "You're too tall, Wilt!"

No matter how he tried, Wilt could not wedge his way in.

Now other youngsters took up the chant. "You're too tall, Wilt! You're too tall!" they jeered.

Indeed, that is the problem.

PUBLISHER'S NOTE

At the end of the 1966-67 season Wilt Chamberlain finally broke the eight-year jinx that had plagued him since his entry into professional basketball—he became a champion on the record books as well as in the hearts of basketball fans and the opinion of experts. The Philadelphia 76ers beat the San Francisco Warriors, 125-122, in the sixth game of the best-of-seven playoff series, to become the NBA champions.

Ironically, both Wilt Chamberlain and the coach of the 76ers, Alex Hannum, were former Warriors. Hannum had been fired by San Francisco after the 1965-66 season and had wound up in Philadelphia. The reunion of the two former Warriors was the best thing that had happened to Philadelphia since Ben Franklin had forsaken the sticks for the big town. Another irony was that the deciding factor in the playoffs was Wilt's defensive play. Since he had left the Warriors, he had become a truly *complete* ballplayer, as devastating on defense as on the attack. In the first five games of the playoffs he had scored only 82 points, but racked up 37 assists and gathered in 148 rebounds. In the final game he was teamed against the Warriors' superstar Rick Barry. Wilt scored 24 points, with four assists and 23 rebounds, and checked Barry so effectively that he was forced off his game. In the final seconds, with the score Philadelphia 123 and San Francisco 122, Barry could see nothing but Chamberlain between him and the basket, and his final shot went wide of the mark. Philadelphia picked up another two points on a foul, and that was the end of the ball game.

Wilt Chamberlain was a champion at last.